Der Geist Issue 6

Editor: Trevor Blake
Co-Editor and Designer: Kevin I. Slaughter
Proof-reader: Fred Woodworth

First Printing: October 2023

Text in a gray box at the head of an article indicates a note from the editors on the article that follows.
The symbol "≠" indicates a footnote original to *Der Geist*.
Section header images by Kevin I. Slaughter.

[Stirner, Max] Blake, Trevor; Kevin I. Slaughter
Perfect bound ISBN 978-1-944651-29-9
Library edition ISBN 978-1-944651-30-5
ISSN 2639-5339
Philosophy
Reference

SUBSCRIPTIONS are not available at press time.
BULK RATES and DISTRIBUTORS and INSTITUTIONS please inquire.

The Union of Egoists publishes original research and rare reprints concerning the philosophy of egoism as published between the years 1845 and 1945. For more information, see...

WEB: UNIONOFEGOISTS.COM

LETTERS/PACKAGES:
Union of Egoists
444 Maryland Ave #7940
Essex, MD 21221

EMAIL: editor@unionofegoists.com

Not responsible for unsolicited materials.

127 House—at every turn in its thought, society will find us waiting.

INTRODUCTION
Trevor Blake & Kevin I. Slaughter   2023

The Union of Egoists brings you *Der Geist*, an anthology of rare and never before seen essays and images from the history of egoism.

This sixth issue of *Der Geist* features the echoes of egoism, the shockwave that emanated from the 1845 publication of *Der Einzige und der Eigentum* by Max Stirner in the philosophical and political press. Those who came after Stirner, such as Malfew Seklew, Ragnar Redbeard, and Dora Marsden, also received rave and raving reviews.

Der Geist offers more than rare reprints, although some of these images and articles have not seen print for generations. This issue contains original translations of egoist items never before rendered into English as well as new bibliographies.

The Union of Egoists has published dozens of books of egoist scholarship, surpassing the study of any number of better-funded, better-staffed efforts. And while my face burns red with bottled-up excitement, I dare not reveal what remains to be released.

Take your time with this issue of *Der Geist* and let us know what you think.

RECENTLY PUBLISHED:

The Radical Book Shop of Chicago: In Which a Disaffected Preacher, His Blind Anarchist Wife, and Their Precocious Daughters Create an Important Hub of Literary, Bohemian, and Revolutionary Culture in Progressive-Era Chicago
Kevin I. Slaughter, with appendix by Lillian Undell
130 pages, 6x9", ISBN 978-1943687-28-2

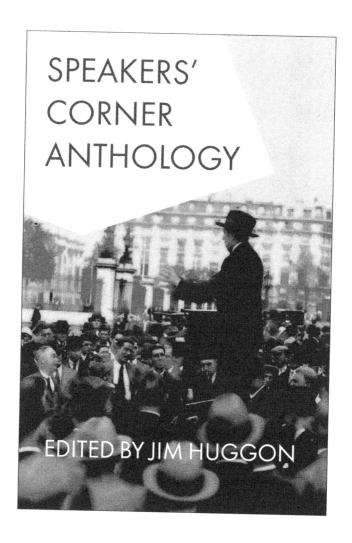

Speakers' Corner Anthology
Edited by Jim Huggon
148 pages, 6x9", ISBN 978-1944651-26-8

The Red Sect
Enzo Martucci
152 pages, 4.25x7", ISBN 978-1-943687-10-7

Recently published:

A Secret Hit: 150 years of Max Stirner's Der Einzige und sein Eigentum
Bernd A. Laska
52 pages, 5.5"x8.5", ISBN 978-1-943687-30-5

MAX STIRNER

Max Stirner (October 25 1806–June 26 1856) was a German philosopher. He is often seen as one of the forerunners of nihilism, existentialism, postmodernism, and anarchism, especially of individualist anarchism. Stirner's main work is *The Ego and His Own* (*Der Einzige und sein Eigentum*). This book is the wellspring of egoism. *Der Einzige* was first published in 1845 in Leipzig, and has since appeared in numerous editions and translations.

> I write because I wish to make for ideas, which are my ideas, a place in the world. If I could foresee that these ideas must take from you peace of mind and repose, if in these ideas that I sow I should see the germs of bloody wars and even the cause of the ruins of many generations, I would nevertheless continue to spread them. It is neither for the love of you nor even for the love of truth that I express what I think. No—I sing! I sing because I am a singer. If I use you in this way, it is because I have need of your ears!
>
> —Max Stirner, *The Ego and His Own*, translated by Steven T. Byington.

Max Stirner's Anarchist Gospel **9**
Current Literature   1907

A Dutch Review of Stirner's Work. **18**
Gustaff Vermeersch   1908

Anarchist Black Dragon **21**
John Bosch and Carl Harp   1981

Max Stirner vs. *Wahrheit-Sucher* **23**
Wahrheit-Sucher   1897

"Celine Adele Marillier". **25**
Edmond-Francois Aman-Jean   1885

Pity and the Future **26**
V. Taubman-Goldie   1914

Max Stirner and the Grisette **27**
Emma Goldman   1913

Steven T. Byington's Triple Score **28**
Trevor Blake   2022

Max Stirner's Anarchist Gospel
Current Literature   1907

From *Current Literature*, Vol. XLII, No. 5, (May 1907). The following review of *The Ego and His Own* was published in Current
Literature. The editor was Edward J. Wheeler: Associate Editors
were Leonard D. Abbot, Alexander Harvey, and George S. Viereck.

Max Stirner's Anarchist Gospel

Sixty years ago, a book entitled *"Der Einzige und sein Eigentum"* (generally translated "The Individual and his Property") was published in
Berlin. It has been described as "the most revolutionary book ever
written," and its author, Max Stirner, was perhaps the leading intellectual precursor of modern philosophical anarchism. When he died,
in 1856, in comparative poverty and obscurity, his theories had made
but little headway; but during the years that have passed since then
both book and author have commanded increasing study and respect.
It begins to look as if Max Stirner might yet take rank with the great
philosophic thinkers of the nineteenth century. He exerted profound
influence over Nietzsche, and, in the opinion of no less an authority
than Eduard von Hartmann, his work surpasses that of Nietzsche
"by a thousand cubits." "Der Einzige" has been translated into French,
Spanish, Russian and Italian; and critical studies popularizing its arguments have appeared in almost all the European countries. George
Brandes, a critic of rare discernment, is one of Stirner's interpreters,
and John Henry Mackay, the German poet, has written his biogra-
phy. On Mackay's initiative a suitable stone has been placed above
Stirner's grave in Berlin, and a memorial tablet upon the house in
which he died; and this spring another tablet is to be set upon the
house in Bayreuth where he was born in 1806.

An English translation of *"Der Einzige,"* which has just appeared
in New York under the title, "The Ego and His Own," makes Stirner's
gospel accessible for the first time to American and English-speaking
readers. He is difficult to read, and his oddities of composition and terminology often tend to obscure his meaning. "There is nothing more
disconcerting," one of his French commentators has confessed, "than
the first approach to this strange work. Stirner does not condescend to

inform us as to the architecture of his edifice, or furnish us the slightest guiding thread.... The apparent divisions of the book are few and misleading. The repetitions are innumerable. At first one seems to be confronted with a collection of essays strung together, with a throng of aphorisms.... But, if you read this book several times; if, after having penetrated the intimacy of each of its parts, you then traverse it as a whole—gradually the fragments weld themselves together, and Stirner's thought is revealed in all its unity, force, and depth."

There are many points of similarity between the philosophies of Stirner and of Nietzsche. Both might take as their creed the ringing lines of Swinburne:

> Honor to man in the highest!
> For man is the master of things.

But while Nietzsche speaks with the inspired accents of a poet, Stirner writes as a philosophical partisan. The former fires the imagination with an essentially aristocratic vision of the "Superman"; the latter proclaims that each individual man is supreme and perfect in himself. Against the opening words of his first chapter, Stirner sets two mottoes, one from Feuerbach, that "man is to man the supreme being"; the other from Bruno Bauer, that "man has just been discovered." He adds the comment: "Then let us take a more careful look at this supreme being and this new discovery."

With a confidence worthy of Carlyle, who once declared that there were twenty-seven million people in England, "mostly fools," Stirner says that when he looks out on the modern world he can only regard the majority of men as "veritable fools, fools in a madhouse." He means that we do not know how to think, how to be ourselves. We take our lives and opinions as they are handed to us; we believe in "spooks" of all kinds; we have "wheels in our heads;" we are all slaves of fixed ideas. It is "fixed ideas" that especially excite Stirner's wrath, and by this term he means ideas of God, marriage, the state, of law, duty, morality. Humanity will only begin to live, he avers, when it gets rid of all fixed ideas.

The trouble with all of us to-day, he asserts, is that we think in crowds, and that our knowledge is alien to us. To follow his argument:

God. Immortality, freedom, humanity, etc., are drilled into

us from childhood, as thoughts and feelings which move our inner being more or less strongly, either ruling us without our knowing it, or sometimes in richer natures manifesting themselves in systems and works of art; but are always not aroused but imparted feelings, because we must believe in them and cling to them....Who is there that has never, more or less consciously, noticed that our whole education is calculated to produce feelings in us, i.e., impart them to us instead of leaving their production to ourselves however they may turn out? If we hear the name of God, we are to feel veneration; if we hear that of the prince's majesty, it is to be received with reverence, deference, submission; if we hear that of morality, we are to think that we hear something inviolable; if we hear of the Evil One or evil ones, we are to shudder, etc. The intention is directed to these feelings, and he who, e.g. should hear with pleasure the deeds of the 'bad' would have to be 'taught what's what' with the rod of discipline. Thus stuffed with imparted feelings, we appear before the bar of majority and are 'pronounced of age.' Our equipment consists of 'elevating feelings, lofty thoughts, inspiring maxims, eternal principles,' etc. The young are of age when they twitter like the old; they are driven through school to learn the old song, and. When they have this by heart, they are declared of age.

We must not feel at everything and every name that comes before us what we could and would like to feel thereat; e.g., at the name of God we must think of nothing laughable, feel nothing disrespectful, it being prescribed and imparted to us what and how we are to feel and think at mention of that name.

That is the meaning of the care of souls,—that my soul or my mind be tuned as others think right, not as I myself would like it. How much trouble does it not cost one finally to secure to one's self a feeling of one's own at the mention of at least this or that name, and to laugh in the face of many who expect from us a holy face and a composed expression at their speeches. What is imparted is alien to us, is not our own, and therefore is 'sacred,' and it is hard work to lay aside the 'sacred dread of it.'

In the terminology of Stirner's subversive gospel, "everything sacred is a tie, a fetter." According to his view of life, all progress consists in the breaking of previously accepted laws. "The history of the world," he says, "shows that no tie has yet remained unrent, that man tirelessly defends himself against ties of every sort." And so he adjures the youth of his age, and of every age, to become rebels, to "practice refractoriness, yes, and complete disobedience." Such adjuration, he is aware, is likely to fall, for the most part, on deaf ears.

One needs only admonish you of yourselves to bring you to despair at once. 'What am I?' each of you asks himself. An abyss of lawless and unregulated impulses, desires, wishes, passions, a chaos without light or guiding star! How am I to obtain a correct answer if, without regard to God's commandments or to the duties which morality prescribes, without regard to the voice of reason, which in the course of history, after bitter experiences, has exalted the best and most reasonable thing into law, I simply appeal to myself? My passion would advise me to do the most senseless thing possible. Thus each deems himself the—devil; for if, so far as he is unconcerned about religion, etc., he only deemed himself a beast, he would easily find that the beast, which does follow only its impulse (as it were, its advice), does not advise and impel itself to do the 'most senseless' things, but takes very correct steps. But the habit of the religious way of thinking has biased our mind so grievously that we are—terrified at ourselves in our nakedness and naturalness ; it has degraded us so that we deem ourselves depraved by nature, born devils. Of course, it comes into your head at once that your calling requires you to do the 'good,' the moral, the right. Now, if you ask yourselves what is to be done, how can the right voice sound forth from you, the voice which points the way of the good, the right, the true, etc.? What concord have God and Belial?

But what would you think if one answered you by saying: 'That one is to listen to God, conscience, duties, laws, etc., is flim-flam with which people have stuffed your head and heart and made you crazy'? And if he asked you how it is that you know so surely that the voice of nature is a seducer? And if he even demanded of you to turn the thing about and actually to deem the voice of God and conscience to be the devil's work? There are such graceless men; how will you settle them? You cannot appeal to your parsons, parents, and good men, for precisely these are designated by them as your seducers, as the true seducers and corrupters of youth, who busily sow broadcast the tares of self-contempt and reverence to God, who fill young hearts with mud and young heads with stupidity.

The real gist of Stirner's argument is already apparent. His logic can have but one eventuation. He challenges men everywhere simply—to be themselves. "I recognize no other source of right," he says, "than me." He continues: "If religion has set up the proposition that we are sinners altogether, I set over against it the other: we are perfect altogether! For we are every moment all that we can be; and we never need be more."

From this it follows that there is no absolute standard of right or wrong. What is right for one man may be wrong for another, and vice versa. Moreover:

A man is 'called' to nothing, and has no 'calling,' no 'destiny,' as little as a plant or a beast has a 'calling.' The flower does not follow the calling to complete itself, but it spends all its forces to enjoy and consume the world as well as it can, — i.e., it sucks in as much of the juices of the earth, as much air of the ether, as much light of the sun, as it can get and lodge. The bird lives up to no calling, but it uses its forces as much as is practicable; it catches beetles and sings to its heart's delight. But the forces of the flower and the bird are slight in comparison to those of a man, and a man who applies his forces will affect the world much more powerfully than flower and beast. A calling he has not, but he has forces that manifest themselves where they are because their being consists solely in their manifestation, and are as little able to abide inactive as life, which, if it 'stood still' only a second, would no longer be life. Now, one might call out to the man, 'use your force.' Yet to this imperative would be given the meaning that it was man's task to use his force. It is not so. Rather, each one really uses his force without first looking upon this as his calling: at all times everyone uses as much force as he possesses. One does say of a beaten man that he ought to have exerted his force more; but one forgets that, if in the moment of succumbing he had had the force to exert his forces (e.g., bodily forces), he would not have failed to do it: even if it was only the discouragement of a minute, this was yet a—destitution of force, a minute long. Forces may assuredly be sharpened and redoubled, especially by hostile resistance or friendly assistance; but where one misses their application one may be sure of their absence, too. One can strike fire out of a stone, but without the blow none comes out; in like manner a man, too, needs 'impact.'

Now, for this reason that forces always of themselves show themselves operative, the command to use them would be superfluous and senseless. To use his forces is not man's calling and task, but is his act, real and extant at all times.

The argument that the world will "go to the dogs" in the moment that each man does as seems best in his own eyes, is met, in part, in Stirner's apostrophe to youth, already quoted. He returns to the point again and again. To those who exclaim, "Society will fall to pieces!" he replies: Men will seek one another as long as they need one another. "But surely one cannot put a rascal and an honest man on the same level!" To this Stirner makes answer:

No human being does that oftener than you judges of morals; yes, still more than that, you imprison as a criminal an honest man who speaks openly against the existing constitution, against the hallowed institutions, etc., and you entrust portfolios and still more important things to a crafty rascal. So in praxi you have nothing to reproach me with. 'But in theory!' Now there I do put both on the same level, as two opposite poles,—to wit, both on the level of the moral law. Both have meaning only in the 'moral' world, just as in the pre-Christian time a Jew who kept the law and one who broke it had meaning and significance only in respect to the Jewish law; before Jesus Christ, on the contrary, the Pharisee was no more than the 'sinner and publican.' So before self-ownership the moral Pharisee amounts to as much as the immoral sinner.

Carrying this startling argument still further, Stirner brands the philanthropists of today as "the real tormentors of humanity." He cries:

> Get away from me with your 'philanthropy'! Creep in, you philanthropist, into the 'dens of vice,' linger awhile in the throng of the great city: will you not everywhere find sin, and sin, and again sin? Will you not wail over corrupt humanity, not lament at the monstrous egoism? Will you see a rich man without finding him pitiless and 'egoistic'? Perhaps you already call yourself an atheist, but you remain true to the Christian feeling that a camel will sooner go through a needle's eye than a rich man not be an 'un-man.' How many do you see anyhow that you would not throw into the 'egoistic mass'? What, therefore, has your philanthropy [love of man] found? Nothing but unlovable men! And where do they all come from? From you, from your philanthropy! You brought the sinner with you in your head, therefore you found him, and therefore you inserted him everywhere. Do not call men sinners, and they are not: you alone are the creator of sinners; you, who fancy that you love men, are the very one to throw them into the mire of sin, the very one to divide them into vicious and virtuous, into men and un-men, the very one to befoul them with the slaver of your possessedness; for you love not men, but man. But I tell you, you have never seen a sinner, you have only—dreamed of him.

"I want to be all and have all that I can be and have." This, says Stirner, is the inevitable basis of conduct. To this we must all come sooner or later. He adds:

> Whether others are and have anything similar, what do I care? The equal, the same, they can neither be nor have. I cause no detriment to them, as I cause no detriment to the rock by being 'ahead of it' in having motion. If they could have it, they would have it.
> To cause other men no detriment is the point of the demand to possess no prerogative; to renounce all 'being ahead,' the strictest theory of renunciation. One is not to count himself as 'anything especial,' such as, e.g., a Jew or

a Christian. Well, I do not count myself as anything espe-
cial, but as unique. Doubtless I have similarity with others;
yet that holds good only for comparison or reflection; in fact,
I am incomparable, unique. My flesh is not their flesh, my
mind is not their mind. If you bring them under the generalities 'flesh, mind,' those are your thoughts, which have
nothing to do with my flesh, my mind, and can least of all
issue a 'call' to mine.

I do not want to recognize or respect in you anything,
neither the proprietor nor the ragamuffin, nor even the man,
but to use you. In salt I find that it makes food palatable to
me, therefore I dissolve it; in the fish I recognize an ailment,
therefore I eat it; in you I discover the gift of making my life
agreeable, therefore I choose you as a companion. Or, in salt
I study crystallization, in the fish animality, in you men, etc.
But to me you are only what you are for me,—to wit, my object; and because my object, therefore my property.

The question arises finally: What is truth? With relentless logic,
Stirner replies: "As long as you believe in the truth you do not believe
in yourself, and are a—servant, a —religious man (that is, a bound
man). You alone are the truth, or, rather, you are more than the truth,
which is nothing at all before you." He says, in concluding:

The truth is dead, a letter, a word, a material that I can use up.
All truth by itself is dead, a corpse; it is alive only in the same
way as my lungs are alive,—to wit, in the measure of my own
vitality. Truths are material, like vegetables and weeds; as to
whether vegetable or weed, the decision lies in me.

Objects are to me only material that I use up. Wherever
I put my hand I grasp a truth, which I trim for myself. The
truth is certain to me, and I do not need to long after it. To
do the truth a service is in no case my intent; it is to me only
a nourishment for my thinking head, as potatoes are for my
digesting stomach, or as a friend is for my social heart. As
long as I have the humor and force for thinking, every truth
serves me only for me to work it up according to my powers.
As reality or worldliness is 'vain and a thing of naught' for
Christians, so is the truth for me. It exists exactly as much as

the things of this world go on existing although the Christian has proved their nothingness; but it is vain, because it has its value not in itself but in me. Of itself it is valueless. The truth is a—creature.

As you produce innumerable things by your activity, yes, shape the earth's surface anew and set up works of men everywhere, so too you may still ascertain numberless truths by your thinking, and we will gladly take delight in them. Nevertheless, as I do not please to hand myself over to serve your newly discovered machines mechanically, but only help to set them running for my benefit, so, too, I will only use your truths, without letting myself be used for their demands.

All truths beneath me are to my liking; a truth above me, a truth that I should have to direct myself by, I am not acquainted with. For me there is no truth, for nothing is more than I!

A Dutch Review of Stirner's Work
Gustaff Vermeersch

1908

From *Den gulden winckel* (February 15, 1908), pp. 27-28. A review of two works by Max Stirner in translation by Jaak Lansen. This review by Gustaff Vermeersch appeared in and is (roughly) translated into English for the first time.

Zevende Jaargang No. 2   15 Februari 1908

DEN·GULDEN·WINCKEL
MAANDSCHRIFT·VOOR·DE·BOEKENVRIENDEN
IN·GROOT·NEDERLAND
ONDER··LEIDING··VAN
GERARD·VAN·ECKEREN
UITGAVE·HOLLANDIA
DRUKKERY··BAARN

RELIGION, WISDOM

MAX STIRNER.—*Het Kersouwken van Ant-M Werpen* has published Max Stirner's work in Dutch. First, his main work appeared: *The One and His Property*. Here we have one of his smaller works: *The False Principle of Our Education or Humanism and Realism*.—The translations are by Jaak Lansen.

It was a good idea for both publisher and translator to offer the works of this forgotten thinker to the Dutch public. Stirner is one of those that must be read, he will gain in fame and followers the more he is read and better understood.

Stirner was more of a romantic than a builder of new systems. To get a system out of work, it must be sought, which is why it is little understood. He is said to be the apostle of the purest egoism; this seems so indeed, and I hope one day to prove otherwise. I particularly value Stirner's cry; he opens up a whole world, as it were. And mankind will one day move in that direction, as the few to whom we owe our great religions. Who could deny the relationship between Stirner and occultism? But our thinking, our insight into things, our purpose in life is so falsified and veiled by interested parties that we shy away from it when the pure truth reveals itself to us.

The False Principle, etc., which is lying here before me, is only a brochure, but its few pages give a lot to think about and lead very far. This booklet is, as it were, a clarification of Stirner's great work, it is more constructive, so it points more clearly where Stirner wanted to go, the goal is very clear to us and it is very correct. This little work was written as a critique on a work by Theodoor Heinsius: Concord between school and life or mediation between Humanism and Realism, from a national point of view, Berlin, 1842 (p. 4). Schrijver follows Heinsius in his brief outline of the course of history. He calls the period between Reformation and Revolution that of the relationship between the mature and the underaged (the mature = the civilized, the underaged = the laity). Before the revolution, he says, civilization was inscribed on the biblical classics. It was the time of the pupils: "We had to get to know form and content (of beauty and truth) first." —"Our own life offered nothing worthy".

This spirit of formalism was resisted. There was no instruction that pertaining to life, and from then on everything had to be known to live, to know to be lived, because only the reality of knowing is a perfection. When they got that far, one had nothing to envy the other, there were no learned gentlemen or ignorant laymen. That is why realism came: "the ability to have a say in everything, more seriously, the ability to master all matter."

"In the meantime, to understand the past, as Humanism teaches, and to grasp the present, as Realism does, both only lead to power over the temporal. Ego is only Spirit, who understands itself. Therefore, equality was given. and freedom only a subordinate existence. One could well be equal to others, and emancipated from their authority; from the equality with oneself, from the equalization and reconciliation of our temporary and present man, from the glorification of our naturalness to spiritualism, in short of the unity and omnipotence of our ego, which has enough of itself, because it leaves nothing strange outside of it; – hardly any foreboding was made of this in said principles. Only Freedom did appear as independence from authorities, but was still empty to self-destiny... "

This quotation gives, briefly, somewhat of Stirner's thoughts on education. "Knowing must die in order to emerge again in death as will". "Not the will is by nature the right thing to do, as the practice and practice would like to assure us, not wanting to jump over knowing – one may, to date. to be with the will, but knowing completes itself to will, when it becomes unconscious, and creates itself as a spirit "that builds itself a body." That is why every education does not cling to this death and this ascension of "knowledge runs out, the defects of temporality, formality and materiality, Dandysm and Industrialism, a knowledge that does not purify and concentrate in such a way that it passes into will." "Only in abstraction does freedom exist: free man only exists he who has conquered what has been given and has himself pulled together what was provoked by him questioningly into the unity of his self".

Where does Stirner want to go? "Raising a creative person instead of a living person." His dream will not be realized for a long time, because for this the whole society must be turned around. In the meantime, reading this work and especially studying it is recommended.

Anarchist Black Dragon
John Bosch and Carl Harp

1981

The *Anarchist Black Dragon* was a prisoner-produced periodical promoting anarchism. In these excerpts, the *ABD* mentions Max Stirner in a positive light. Source spelling retained.

Terrorism

by John Bosch and Carl Harp
Anarchist Black Dragon
Washington State Penitentiary
Number 8 (February 14 1981) page 15

The idea that terrorism results from the Capitalistic sickness(es) of individualism is false. Individualism is neither a sickness nor is it a result of Capitalism. The Capitalists might talk big about the right of a person to be an individual, but in actual practice they deny this right to anyone but themselves. Even amoung themselves, there are strict rules of behaviour that dictate just how for one may go in practicing it.

The only ones who actively pursue Individualism are the Egoists and other types of anarchist. The fundamental concepts of Anarchism are Individualism and related ideas. Max Stirner presented the idea in The Ego and Its Own. All other Anarchist theories revolve around this basic concept, that the individual has the right to dictate his own life.

Misdirected acts are a danger and a symptom (sometimes) of ir-responsibility, but we must recognize the right of all people to use whatever weapons are available to them. Survival is often a rationale for using terrorism. Terror, properly used, is one of the best psyco-logical weapons in any arsenal. Let no one disarm the people...

"Freedom You Want..."

Max Stirner
Anarchist Black Dragon
Washington State Penitentiary
Volume 1 Number 11 (circa March 1983)

Freedom you want, you want freedom. Why then do you higgle over a more or less? Freedom can only be the whole of freedom; a piece of freedom is not freedom. You despair of the possibility of obtaining the whole of freedom, freedom from everything, yes, you consider it insanity even to wish this? Well, then leave off chasing after the phantom, and spend your pains on something better than the unattainable. Therefore turn to yourselves rather than to your gods or idols, Bring out from yourselves what is in you, bring it to the light, bring yourselves to revelation. How one acts only from himself, and asks after nothing further, the Christians have realized in the notion "God. " He acts "as it pleases him." And foolish man, who could do just so, is to act as it "pleases God" instead. If it is said that even God proceeds according to eternal laws, that too fits me, since I too cannot get out of my skin, but have my law in my whole nature, i.e. in myself.

If your efforts are ever to make freedom the issue, then exhaust freedom's demands, Who is it that is to be come free? You, I, we. Free from what? From everything that is not you, not I, not we. I, therefore, am the kernel that is to be delivered from all wrappings and freed from all cramping shells. What is left when I have been freed from everything that is not I? Only I; nothing but I. But freedom has nothing to offer this I himself. As to what is now to happen further after I have become free, freedom is silent, as our governments, when the prisoner's time is up, merely let him go, thrusting him out into abandorment.

The State has nothing to be more afraid of than the value of me, and no thing must it more carefully guard against than every occasion that offers itself to me for realizing value from myself. What a slave will do as soon as he has broken his fetters, one must await...

Max Stirner vs. *Wahrheit-Sucher*
Wahrheit-Sucher   **1897**

From *Wahrheit-Sucher* Vol. 1 No. 8 (February 1897). Interest in, support for, or antagonism against the works of Max Stirner are found where they are found, not always where one might expect to find them. Here we see a critical mention of *Der Einzige und sein Eigentum* in an occult journal whose title translates as "The Truth Seeker." This letter to the editor from Max Seiling is in response to an article by J. Peve. An original translation from the Union of Egoists.

Since it is absolutely impossible for a person to act against his or her well-being and interest, since all human actions arise from selfishness, I can have a "selflessness" in which one harms the other without the slightest advantage of it being introduced. Because, assuming that it really did happen (there are certainly no "countless amount" of such cases) if someone would willingly and happily sacrifice his or her life or belongings in order to harm another person, he would just be able to do so by his devilish character, his or her enjoyment of malicious joy being higher than life and good; at least he would have achieved an advantage, albeit a few that could be understood. How Mr. Peve, after only wanting to accept this case as actual "selflessness", can finally say: "I am beyond all selflessness and domination," is unclear to me. The final remark that "selfishness alone corresponds to reason" is reminiscent of the teachings of the now so-called Nietzsche and his predecessor Stirner, who with his book *The Ego and His Own* exalting the glorification of selfishness. Instead of going into this in more detail immediately, I would like to briefly present my own point of view on the extremely important question of the ethical value of human actions. It then emerges automatically what value the so-called selfish actions.

Max Stirner

"Celine Adele Marillier"
Edmond-Francois Aman-Jean   1885

On October 2, 2013, the Dallas Auction Gallery listed the following:

Edmond-Francois Aman-Jean, "Celine Adele Marillier" oil on canvas, 1885. Signed and inscribed in gold upper right "Anno – MDCCCLXXXV / Aman Jean pinxit / Imago Celine Adele Marillier / Aetatis Suae / XXV". Canvas: 45.5"H x 35.5"W; Frame: 50"H x 40"W. Provenance: Christie's London, June 25 1998, Lot 292. Note: Accompanied by a photocertificate signed by Robert Hellebranth, dated April 23, 1998, stating this work will be included in the artist's catalogue raisonne. The book held by the sitter is *L'unique et sa propriete* by Max Stirner, originally published in German in 1845 as *Der einzige und sein eigentum*. An extract from the book is inscribed on the stretcher verso. Edmond-Francois Aman-Jean (French, 1860-1935) was known for his landscapes and female portraits.

We have reproduced the work on the facing page. The Union of Egoists is keen on contacting the current owner of this piece.

Pity and the Future
V. Taubman-Goldie

From *The Suffragette* (April 24, 1914). A plea for pity in the face of the battalions of Friedrich Nietzsche and Max Stirner. Valentine Francis Goldie-Taubman (1875 – ?) was an author.

They say—the practical, unsentimental folk—that this attitude of sympathy cannot last; that by our own showing the possession of power petrifies the heart; that it is the subjected position of women that makes them gentler by nature; and that once admitted to equal rights with man, they will inevitably become equally callous. It may be so; it may be that the world will one day become wholly populated by disciples of Nietzsche and Max Stirner, in which case my only consolation is that I shall be comfortably cremated before this age is reached. But I do not believe it: I think that the time IS at hand when society is ready for fellowship, and that it only needs a big shake-up, the destruction of an age-old tyranny, to begin to usher in the new era. At least, woman's freedom seems to me our last chance of re-moulding the world nearer to the heart's desire of myself and those who think with me. The battalions of the Parsifalites and the *Also-sprach-Zarathustrans* are already mustering for the encounter; and it is to the newly armed, pity-enlightened squadrons of my sisters that I look for the victor.

Max Stirner and the Grisette

Emma Goldman

1913

Emma Goldman (1869 – 1940) was an anarchist of the collective variety, but she knew her individualist anarchists too. In *Victims of Morality and The Failure of Christianity* (1913) Goldman gets personal about Max Stirner and his darling in Goldman's denunciation of morality.

The term "grisette", when used by English writers, usually referred to a young lady who was employed in a city either as a clerk, seamstress, or prostitute. Sometimes she is depicted as being both working in a service job and being a prostitute. If she was not a prostitute, she was considered flirtatious or sexually available. She is personified as Rigolette in Eugene Sue's *The Mysteries of Paris*, a book Stirner wrote a review of. This review may be the source of Goldman's reference.

Meanwhile the respectable young man, excited through the daily association and contact with his sweetheart, seeks an outlet for his nature in return for money. In ninety-nine cases out of a hundred, he will be infected, and when he is materially able to marry, he will infect his wife and possible offspring. And the young flower, with every fiber aglow with the fire of life, with all her being crying out for love and passion? She has no outlet. She develops headaches, insomnia, hysteria; grows embittered, quarrelsome, and soon becomes a faded, withered, joyless being, a nuisance to herself and everyone else. No wonder Stirner preferred the grisette to the maiden grown gray with virtue.

Steven T. Byington's Triple Score
Trevor Blake   2022

Steven T. Byington created the first full English translation of *Der Einzige und sein Eigentum*, published in 1907.

Max Stirner wrote in *Der Einzige und sein Eigentum* (1845):

Byington translation in *The Ego and His Own* (1907):

Wie bei den Griechen möchte man den Menschen jetzt zu einem zoon politikon machen, einem Staatsbürger oder politischen Menschen. So galt er lange Zeit als »Himmelsbürger«. Der Grieche wurde aber mit seinem Staate-zugleich entwürdigt, der Himmelsbürger wird es mit dem Himmel; Wir hingegen wollen nicht mit dem Volke, der Nation und Nationalität zugleich untergehen, wollen nicht bloss politische Menschen oder Politiker sein. »Volksbeglückung« strebt man seit der Revolution an, und indem man das Volk glücklich, gross u. dergl. macht, macht man Uns unglücklich: Volksglück ist—mein Unglück.

As with the Greeks, there is now a wish to make man a *zoon politicon*, a citizen of the State or political man. So he ranked for a long time as a "citizen of heaven." But the Greek fell into ignominy along with his State, the citizen of heaven likewise falls with heaven; we, on the other hand, are not willing to go down along with the people, the nation and nationality, not willing to be merely political men or politicians. Since the Revolution they have striven to "make the people happy," and in making the people happy, great, etc., they make Us unhappy: the people's good hap is—my mishap.

Byington was able to convey the double-meaning of Stirner in "...the Greek fell into ignominy along with his *State*... " because in English, State can refer both to "nation" and "nature." Byington also conveyed the deliberate ambiguity of the capitalized "Us" in the final sentence: it is "us" the people they strive to make happy, and "Us" the Royal singular who are not made happy, both at the same time as a deliberate contradiction. But Byington scores a triple goal with closing alliteration. See the poetry of **hap**py / un**hap**py (favorable / unfavorable mood), **hap** (circumstance) and mis**hap** (accident).

MALFEW SEKLEW

Sirfessor F. W. Wilkesbarre (aka Malfew Seklew) was born in Great Britain in the 1860s. In the 1890s and early 1900s he was a contributor to and associate editor to *The Eagle and The Serpent*. Sirfessor came to the United States in 1916. He shared an address with Ragnar Redbeard in Chicago in 1927, the year Seklew wrote *The Gospel According to Malfew Seklew*. By the 1930s he was living in New York City. He died in 1938.

> Are you a Simpoleon or a Supercrat? A Peter-pantheist or a Personality? Are you a Bromide or a Sulphide? A nonentity or a reality? Are you an unripe ego or an unfinished organism with underdone understanding and hard boiled beliefs, pingpong principles and petrified prejudices? Do you amble through the atmosphere with the courage of a carrot, the consciousness of a cabbage, the turpitude of a turnip, the pep of a prune, the punch of a parsnip and the psychology of a Sundowner in the swamps of Hobohemia, or do you dash through space with the courage of a Conqueror and the wisdom of a Will-to-Power Man? If not, massage your Mentoids, and be saved—from yourself at your worst.
>
> —Sirfessor F. W. Wilkesbarre,
> *The Gospel According to Malfew Seklew*

On "Bernard's Tour" 31
Malfew Seklew   1898

Minister Mocks Malfew. 34
Walter Higgins   1907

Stern Critique of Christian Socialist 37
Malfew Seklew   1909

Seklew Asks: Nietzsche to Blame? 39
R. Spencella McGean   1914

Social Aristocrat Socialist Secretary 41
David Nicholls   1909

A Freak Among Reformers 43
The Clarion   1902

No Guide for Anybody. 44
The Sunday Referee   1899

Proletarians in Purgatory 45
Justice   1902

No *Justice* for Malfew Seklew 46
Justice   1902

"We're All More or Less Nutty" 47
The Kansas City Times   1928

Not Seeking Work 48
Malfew Seklew   1906

Seklew Scolds Simpoleons... 49
Malfew Seklew   1914

No Detail Too Small! 50
Trevor Blake   2023

On "Bérnard's Tour"
Malfew Seklew   1898

From *Freedom* (August 1, 1898), p. 55. The following "scene report" was published under the section header "The Propaganda" and the sub-title of "Bérnard's Tour." Originally signed "M.W.", it shows Sirfessor Wilkesbarre's signature style, including the phrase "demigod of the demidamned" which is unlikely to be penned by anyone else. Malfew Seklew, like his pal Ragnar Redbeard, was a man of many names. William Francis Bérnard was a poet who contributed works to *Free Society* (1897), *Lucifer, the Light Bearer* (1883), *The Agitator* (1910), *Liberty* (1881), *Mother Earth* (1906) and other radical journals of the day. S. E. Parker relates that Bérnard was the editor of *The Truthseeker*, a secularist journal published in Bradford by J. W. Gott. Gott was imprisoned for Blasphemy, and it seems Bérnard may have stood in for a time. The history of that small journal is unclear.

In Manchester, on Sunday July 3rd, Bérnard spoke in the afternoon in Stevenson Square — in fact, made his debut as an outdoor speaker here. He did well and agreeably surprised us all. I also spread myself in my own way for about twenty minutes, and also at night at the New Cross; Bérnard did not attend this meeting. His meeting at the Forum went fairly well; he disturbed the equinamity of the mentally-maimed mugwumps and Semitic sycophants who assembled there. Anarchists, said one Semitic speaker, were not wanted there; they were too respectable to listen to such tommy-rot as Anarchism.

Portrait of William F. Barnard, originally published in *To-Morrow*, Vol.1 No. 11, November 1905.

Bérnard is making a good impression wherever he goes, so far; and if he could be prevailed upon to stick to out-door propaganda would be still greater force for good. He spoke three times last week (Tuesday, Wednesday and Thursday evenings) on "Government" at the Monolith; twice yesterday (Sunday 10th), in the morning at the Monolith and in the afternoon at the Hall of Science on the platform made famous by Charles Bradlaugh; in both lectures government in all its ramifications being criticised unmercifully.

The visit of W.F. Bérnard to Bradford will be remembered by many for a long time ; for it is the beginning of a new epoch for reformers. His first lecture at Laycock's Coffee House lecture hall was filled to overflowing, enough turned away to fill the place over again. His lecture was on government: he proved that government per se is exploitation; that it lives on what it steals from the producers, and that is essentially the domination of the stronger over the weaker; that it could not be improved so that it could become innocuous, but must be annihilated, as a cancer in the body must be annihilated if one is to be cured. Government is the cancer of the body politic and must be destroyed before the people or the individual can be free. Government is the root of all evil, that abounds in society today. It creates monopolies, makes criminals and punishes, as Huxley once said, "men for trying to be natural beings." For the people in jail are there for violation of statute law, which is in itself a violation of natural law. Law creates disorder, chaos and charity. Law is for the plunderers of the people, the privileged classes; it conserves their robberies, preserves their privileges, protects their pleasures and is the instrument that enables the parasites of society to fleece and flim and flam the proletariat scientifically—so insidiously and so subtly that the people don't know it. Law, like religion, was invented to make people contented, submissive and humble. Politicians are parasites and professional purloiners of the peoples productions.

The House of Commons is a den of thieves, as Cobbett once said; government is fundamentally the cause of all misery, suffering, poverty, destitutions and crime rampant in our midst.

The tin gods of the reformers, the leading lights of those hyphenated hybrids the Social Democrats and the mildew-minded members of the Single Tax school of rainbow-chasers and foam fighters rose in the wrath and tried to counteract the influence of the logical and analytical presentations of Bérnard. One great man, who is considered at Laycock's an orator, a scholar and a critic, asked if Gladstone—the good, the great and the grand—was like unto these politicians described by the lecturer. Gladstone the G.O.M. (meaning the Grand Old Mugwamp, an apt and true title, was an amateur in everything except politics. He was a mediocrity with a good memory, and expert politician who understood his trade thoroughly; and, therefore, was a consummate bamboozler of the people. Altogether Bérnard pulled down this demigod of the demidamned, Gladstone, from his pedestal and placed this papier-mache hero before the audience in his true character as a fluent phrasemonger, a superb straddler and a magnificent manipulator of the masses. He will be remembered by the posterity as a carnivorous animal with heavenly hallucinations, famous as a majestic masticator of meat (chewing his meat 29 times before swallowing, as recorded in the papers), a vigorous and virile chopper of wood and a man who had the audacity to part his name, like his principles, exactly in the centre—like a bicyclist who parts his hair in the centre to better maintain his equilibrium.

Altogether, but tell it not in Gath, Bérnard flagellated the arguments of the fanatical fossils into fragments and left these deluded decadents wailing and declaiming against the treatment their dogmas, delusions and deities had received at his hands. It was a sight for the gods to see these poor things suffer so severely.

On the night following, Monday, at the request of the several members Bérnard was urged to deliver his view re the way to economic salvation. He did so. The hall was again crowded; and he made quite an innovation in dealing with the subject. He took Communist Anarchist view and the Individualist Anarchist conception, graphically depicting both methods, which appeared to interest the audience. The great men of this locality scintillated but poorly in opposition and the lights went out after much light had been thrown on this vexed yet vital subject. We collected 18s., sold many papers and pamphlets of all kinds and were ably assisted by Mr. John Hacking, Mr. Kay, Mr. Tom Joy and Mr. J. W. Gott, the clothier, and founder and proprietor of the *Truthseeker*. He gave 6s. and entertained Bérnard and me at his house. He is a good fellow.

Minister Mocks Malfew
Walter Higgins
1907

From *Labour Leader* (July 5 1907). A piece of purple progressive prose propaganda makes fun of Sirfessor Malfew Seklew in the emphasis-added section.

THE PRODIGAL SON

It was Sunday evening, about nine o'clock, in the year nineteen hundred and anything you like. The Vicar, his wife and family, together with Sir Jasper Claddon, their intimate and wealthy friend, had just returned from church, and were about to settle down for supper.

"John," said the Vicar's wife in a high-pitched, toneless voice, generally known as "aristocratic," "have I heard that sermon before ?"

"I don't know, my dear; I have preached it fifteen times."

"In your own church, John?"

"Don't ask so many questions, my dear; you are really–"

"But it's a splendid sermon for all that," interrupted Sir Jasper." It's one of those that cannot be repeated too often or too strongly. The more these 'reformers' are shown up and denounced from our pulpits the better for good old England. I was immensely struck with your eloquent exposure of these fearful Socialists. In my opinion, Socialism is the anti-Christ mentioned in the Gospels."

The Vicar's wife shuddered. All were attentive, Socialism being to them an interesting though repulsive subject. Sir Jasper continued:

"I reckon the world's going Socialist mad! Socialist mad!" he repeated. "Fancy preaching that all men are equal." He turned to the butler who had just entered the room, "Why, Simpson, they'll be saying next that we're as good as each other."

"Yes, sir," said Simpson, softly; "the thing's absurd on the face of it."

"What do you mean?" snapped Sir Jasper, not quite sure of Simpson's tone.

"Just what you said, sir." And Simpson withdrew quietly.

"I cannot think what the world is coming to. Things didn't happen like this at one time," said the Vicar. "I remember the time when working men used to come to hear me preach."

"Some few years ago that," said the Vicar's son, a bright, open-faced lad of some twenty summers.

"And the point about it all is," continued the Vicar; "we're power-less to move in the matter. Ever since they stopped plural voting, and abolished the House of Lords, and disestablished the Church, we've had no say. It's absolute tyranny."

"Why don't you rebel?" suggested the son, with a laugh. "Band yourselves together, and form a **Social Aristocratic Federation**, or an *Independent Leisure Party*, and hold **meetings in Hyde Park**, and have processions, and go and storm the Labour Churches, and raid the House of Commons."

"And be sent to prison like the suffragettes in the olden days," said the Vicar's eldest daughter, scornfully. "I really believe you sympathise with these awful people."

"I do—with all my big heart."

"What?" thundered the Vicar; "you sympathise with Socialists? I thought I'd educated you."

"You have, father."

"Do you mean to tell me –" began Sir Jasper, testily.

"I mean to tell you—that I am a Socialist."

Sir Jasper gasped for breath, his face assuming a purple hue: words failed him for some moments. "And you think you're going to marry my daughter?" Once more he paused involuntarily.

"This grieves me more than you can think," said the Vicar. "I always thought you were going to be a missionary."

All eyes regarded the boy.

"Don't mistake me, father," he said. "I am going to be a missionary. Never for one instant have I lost sight of that; never for one instant have I realised the need of that more than now. The heathen are in gross darkness. I will go among them and show them the Light of the World. And they shall follow that Light, that shineth more and more unto the perfect day. I will preach to them, will work. I will set before them the Truth, the Truth that shall make them free. And they shall be sanctified through Truth. I will reveal to them the Way, the only Living Way, the Way of Salvation, that leadeth unto Life."

The Vicar sighed. "That's better, my boy: I like to hear you talk like that." A tear trickled down the mother's cheek. Sir Jasper beamed.

"The one passionate desire of my life is to be a missionary. Oh, how they need someone—the poor, sunken, benighted, degraded pieces of humanity."

"Too true!" The Vicar shook his head, dolefully.

"And I start to-morrow," announced the boy, suddenly.

"What?" came the astonished chorus.

"You're going abroad to-morrow?" cried the mother, terror-stricken.

"Abroad?" asked the son. "Who said anything about going abroad?"

"But the missionary work?"

"The heathens I begin to convert to-morrow are father's congregation. The Way, the Truth, and the Life, that I shall teach them is Socialism."

A period of profound and eloquent silence preceded the burst of the storm.

Stern Critique of Christian Socialist

Malfew Seklew   1909

From *The Haslingden Gazette* (November 20, 1909). Sirfessor
Malfew Seklew, the Man Without a Soul, the Laughing
Philosopher, soundly cleaves Christianity from Socialism in this
letter to the editor.

TO THE EDITOR OF THE *GAZETTE*:

Sir:

I see you have a Mrs. Grundy in trousers on the growl and a
Puritan on the prowl, prancing through your columns under the
verdant name of "F. Green." This individual seems to me to be a re-
incarnation of "Praise God Barebones," tinctured with the spirit of
the Inquisitors of Spain. If such men as F. Green ruled England all
freedom-loving creatures would hasten away to other lands, or be
compelled to commit suicide to escape from the misery and monoto-
ny of "Merrie England." Happily, however, such men have little power
today even in this country, outside the jails, the workhouses, and the
insane asylums, and I hope and trust that men like F. Green — dominated by the furies of fanaticism — will never have an opportunity
to exhibit their atavistic tendencies to the disadvantage of saner and
more humane men and women.

There appears to be much misunderstanding the minds of
the "Great Unhatched" among the "Great Unwashed" concerning
Christianity and Socialism. Christianity and Socialism are distinct
and separate from each other. No true Christian can be a Socialist if
he accepts the Bible as his standard of duty, and is content to remain
in the position it has pleased God to put him.

Socialism teaches the reverse of this. The Socialist glorifies
discontent, and yearns to reconstruct Government, and through
Government, thus relegating God to the background and displaying
his belief that environment — plus natal influence — is the moulder
of man. No sane Socialist, therefore, can be a Christian. The reason
why there is so much difference in the definitions of Socialism is because some are dominated by dogma, some by emotion, and a few
by reason. There are three big battalions in the army of Socialists.
The first is the Social Democratic Party, which advocates the Gospel

according to Karl Marx — plus politics. The second is the Independent Labour Party, which is dominated by Keir Hardie and Co. and politics — plus Socialism. The third is the Christian Social Union — or Christian Socialist — who is dominated by sentiment — plus heavenly hallucinations. The first two owe their origin and present position to the labour of Atheists.

The S.D.F. is founded on the teachings of two Atheists (Karl Marx and Frederick Engels), fostered and sustained by the work of two propagandists, H. M. Hyndman and Harry Quench, Editor of "Justice," the organ of Social Democracy. The I.L.P. is practically the outcome of the writings of Robert Blatchford, the Atheistic author of "Not Guilty" and "God and my Neighbour"; and Keir Hardie.

The Christian Socialists are merely sentimental yearnists and municipal moanists, who have entered the Socialist arena since Socialism became popular among the working classes.

This demonstrates beyond peradventure that Socialism owes nothing to Christianity or Christians, and reconciles some people to the belief that no honest-minded thinker can truthfully say he is a Socialist and a Christian.

MALFEW SEKLEW.
President of the Society of Social Aristocrats.

Seklew Asks: Nietzsche to Blame?
R. Spencella McGean   1914

From *T. P.'s Weekly* Volume 24, Number 628 (November 21, 1914), p. 560. A previously unknown letter to the editor by one "R. Spencella McGean," strongly suspected to be the Mrs. of Sirfessor Malfew Seklew. This letter lists several other significant egoist authors, translators and publishers, as well as making the bold claim that Sirfessor Seklew was the first to present Nietzsche to an English-speaking audience.

To the Editor of *T.P.'s WEEKLY.*
SIR,—

Our Society has been very much interested in your articles on Nietzsche, and feels indebted to Mr. Holbrook Jackson for his lucid and remarkably unbiassed article on this advocator of the Superman and the Super-Race. It has been Nietzsche's misfortune to have been born in an age when morality was so rampant as to obscure the psychic vision of even clear thinkers. There have, however, been a few who have appreciated his philosophy. Of these, our President, Malfew Seklew, has been one, and we venture to submit to you and your readers a small account of his efforts in this direction:—

I have been a reader of *T.P.'s WEEKLY* ever since the first number, and nothing has interested me more than Mr. Holbrook Jackson's article on 'The Truth about Nietzsche.' It gives me pleasure to see so influential a force as *T.P.'s WEEKLY* giving recognition to the labours of Irwin McCall [sic], the editor of *The Eagle and the Serpent*, and of Thomas Common.

Through the medium of *The Truthseeker*, a monthly journal published in Bradford, I introduced the public to flashes of lightning from the pen of Nietzsche. In most of the large centres of England and Scotland I introduced the gospel of the Superman and Social Aristocracy, ably assisted by Mr. Thomas Common. In the coffee taverns, where debates are held, the same thing was done. The Cogers Society of London, where the cranks of the Metropolis used to congregate;

Lester's Coffee House of Nottingham, which Robert Owen used to frequent; Laycock's Coffee Tavern of Bradford, the Talking Shop of Yorkshire, where all sorts of saints and sinners have assembled for forty years to discuss the Desires of Demos, have all been scenes of wordy warfare in the introduction of the Gospel of Nietzsche. In the County Forum of Manchester, also, I was the first to introduce this strange philosophy.

As President of the Society of Social Aristocracy, of which I am the founder, I have so irritated and irrigated the minds of the mindful with alliterative phrases and sound philosophy that many of them have at last commenced to think—for themselves.

Possibly the above may interest your readers, and if anyone is interested in Irwin McCall [sic] or Ragnar Redbeard, Mr. Seklew is in personal touch with these gentlemen and will be glad to give their addresses if desired.

—Yours, etc.,
The Society of Social Aristocrats and Conscious Egoists.
R. SPENCELLA McGEAN,
Secretary.

Social Aristocrat Socialist Secretary
David Nicholls   1909

From *The Haslingden Gazette* (November 27, 1909). This breathless atheist screed from David Nicholls not only uses some of the
standard stock sayings of Sirfessor Malfew Seklew, but identifies
Nicholls as the Secretary of Seklew's Society of Social Aristocrats
and Conscious Egoists.

You deserve the hearty thanks of all Socialists for the courageous
way in which you are allowing a discussion of the differences we have
with Christians. Without apology, I will give your readers some reasons why we reject Christianity. We reject Christianity because it is
the evangel of self-abnegation, instead of self-realization; self-oblit-
eration instead of self-assertion; also because it glorifies altruism,
duty, humility, submission, contentment, and other slave virtues.
We believe Christianity to be the cause of the decadence of the common people, and for the existence of this respectable barbarism, er-
roneously described as "civilisation." Civilisation is not worth having
where the wants of the individual are not satisfied. For what is civilization if it brings not happiness? For this we reject Christianity. We
reject Christianity because we think it is responsible for this pseu-
do-civilisation, with its corroding charity, its cant, hypocrisy, wage
slavery, the sybaritic splendor of the parasites and the squalid misery
of the producer. We reject it because it is founded on a myth, built
round a nonentity — like Santa Claus — who never lived, except in
the imagination of hare-brained hierarchs, deluded decadents, persons suffering from hypothetical nebulosity, and a few others who
are afflicted with sympathetic diarrhea. We believe Christianity to be
a curse and incubus on the minds of the mutable many. For this we
reject it. We repudiate Christianity and all other theorems that quail
under the staunch, steadfast gaze of reason and scientific analysis.
We reject it because its devotees have ever been the enemies of progress and the proletariat; because it is founded on fiction, not fact —
blindfold belief, not judgment, knowledge or reason. Christianity has
ever been the foe of those benefactors, liberty, learning and love. We
reject it because it demoralizes the minds of the demi-damned, the
workers; chloroforms the conceptions of womankind, and confuses

and confounds the brains of the young.

David Nicholl (Sec.), Society of Social Aristocrats and Conscious Egoists. 19 Welbeck Street, Gorton, Manchester.

[Note: we have been compelled to curtail our correspondent's letter somewhat. – ed.]

Burnley Express

D. Nicholl, "Secretary of the Social Aristocrats and Conscious Egoists," 22 Northside Terrace, Bradford, writes explaining why Socialists reject Christianity, which, Mr. Nicholl says, is "the gospel for rainbow chasers, snobocrats, sucklings, slaves, and sycophants. So we leave it to them. We want none of it."

A Freak Among Reformers
The Clarion   1902

From *The Clarion* (September 26, 1902). Glasgow Green is the oldest park in the city of Glasgow, established in the fifteenth century. It was during an amble in the Green in 1765 that James Watt conceived of the condenser for the steam engine, the key concept creating the Industrial Revolution. In this letter, an altogether different set of discoveries is disclosed. Sirfessor Seklew sings the praises of his own essay in *The Eagle and the Serpent* (which he himself humbly edited). He likewise lauds *Liberty Luminants*.

ON TOUR
The Malfew Seklew Egoist-Socialist Propaganda Co.

Malfew Seklew, lecturer; Erwin McCall, advertising manager; J. W. Gott, treasurer; W. Barrie, secretary. MALFEW SEKLEW, the New Apostle of the New Gospel, the New Crusader of Egoistic Socialism, the Originator of Immoral Socialism, the Inventor of the New Method of Propagating the New Thought of New Socialism, and the Expounder of the New Individualism and Scientific Egoism, will lecture, Sunday next and following Sunday, on Glasgow Green, at 2 p.m. and 6 p.m. Babes and sucklings, creeplings and christlings, stay away. All others invited. No collection. Discussion open to anybody on two legs–of the genus *homo*. First spasm: "Altruism Crucified." Second spasm: "The Missing Link in the Solution of the Social Problem." Third spasm: "Why Socialism Does Not Grow / Egoism the Dawn of Liberty." Hear Malfew Seklew, the iconoclastic, atheistic, hedonistic and egoistic Socialist, with Anarchist proclivities, tell the tale; and see Mrs. Grundy sobbing bitterly as this freak among reformers unclothes his thoughts in the open air. £20 offered to the first logical refutation of the arguments advanced in the article "Egoism: Conscious and Unconscious." £2 will be given to the best answer to same. See *Eagle and Serpent* for September, 2d. post free. Read *Liberty Luminants*, the New Bible for Reformers, 72 pages, 3d. post free. Apply to W. Barrie c/o D. Baxter, 126, Trongate, Glasgow.

No Guide for Anybody
The Sunday Referee   **1899**

From *The Sunday Referee* (October 8, 1899). Malfew Seklew, author and subject of the *Gospel of Malfew Seklew*, is taken to task in this uncredited essay. At the time Sirfessor Seklew was the editor of *The Truthseeker* magazine. The uncredited author here predicts that *The Truthseeker* would not last. I write now of the Laughing Philosopher and *The Truthseeker* is published to this very day; The *Sunday Referee* and its Handbooker Clubs closed shop in the 1930s and the author of this essay is unknown.

It is very interesting to learn that there is a Handbooker Club in Newcastle-on-Tye, and that its members meet on Sunday evenings to discuss the matter furnished by those columns. The secretary of the club invites me to an expression of my views on Egoism and Altruism, mainly, as I gather, in the hope that I might assist the members in combating the views of Mr. Malfew Seklew, editor of the *Truthseeker*, of Bradford. I have very little space at my disposal at this moment, but the club secretary sends me two copies of the journal in question, and enables me to form some judgment of Mr. Seklew's value as an intellectual guide. I learn from a glance at page 5 of No. 6 of the *Truthseeker*, over Mr. Seklew's signature, that so long as a dog on the wheel of progress buries its head in the shifting sands of sentiment, it will remain insipid and insane, instead of being a soldier foremost in the ranks of freedom. I am informed that the members of the Handbooker Club are all young men, and I would very earnestly counsel them to notice that this kind of confusion is never encountered in the writing of any person who has ever begun to study the art of thinking. There is nothing which betrays the muddle-headed more fatally than the jumble of incongruous [things]. A writer who thinks he thinks whilst his mental images are involved in that kind of chaos is no guide for anybody.

Proletarians in Purgatory

Justice   **1902**

From *Justice* (August 9, 1902). Sirfessor Malfew Seklew takes on the Social Democratic Federation.

DEBATE, Sunday, August 10, at 6.30 p.m., on "Meadows," Edinburgh, between GEORGE DOULL (S.D.F.) and MALFEW SEKLEW (the Apostle of Atheogism), on "Why the Proletarians are in Purgatory."

ANARCHISTS IN EDINBURGH.

DEAR COMRADE,

In your last issue appears a letter signed L. Vyner, Edinburgh, who expressed a wish therein that some representative of the S.D.F. might join issue in the Meadows with the "blatant egoist" named Malfew Seklew, who takes pleasure in ridiculing Social-Democracy, and take advantage of the big crowds Seklew gets to spread our principles. If I mistake not this is an attempt on the part of Seklew and his friends to draw attention to themselves and their meetings, and to get a bigger crowd by this "draw." Readers of JUSTICE possibly might infer from Vyner's letter that the Social-Democrats of Edinburgh had been frightened into silence by the blatant and egoistic one. Now, as a matter of fact, on the night Vyner speaks of, Malfew Seklew got as unmerciful drubbing from our comrade Doull, of the Edinburgh branch, as it was ever the fate of an Anarchist to receive at the hands of a class-conscious Socialist. I hope you will insert this and expose an attempt on the part of the Anarchists above mentioned to obtain cheap advertisement and a further draw.

Fraternally yours,
R. R. O'CONNOR.
Edinburgh.

L. VINER writes: "I am grievously disappointed. After all my trouble of last week, not a single S.D.F. member came out to uphold our principles in defiance of Malfew Seklew, who claims to be the apostle of Atheogism, the new religion of reason. We need a good, strong man to counteract his influence. I may say there is rumour that our local champion, Mr. Doull, will combat him at his next meeting."

No *Justice* for Malfew Seklew
Justice

1902

From *Justice* (August 9, 1902). Malfew Seklew is taken to task in this letter to the editor by R. R. O'Conner. We were already aware of letters to the editor warning of the impossibility of defeating the Sirfessor in debate–but here we have an accusation that it is the Sirfessor himself who is the author of those letters. Also found here is a notice for an upcoming debate between Seklew and a contender.

ANARCHISTS IN EDINBURGH

DEAR COMRADE,

In your last issue appears a letter signed L. Vyner, Edinburgh, who expressed a wish therein that some representative of the S.D.F. might join issue in the Meadows with the "blatant egoist" named Malfew Seklew, who takes pleasure in ridiculing Social-Democracy, and take advantage of the big crowds Seklew gets to spread our principles. If I mistake not this is an attempt on the part of Seklew and his friends to draw attention to themselves and their meetings, and to get a bigger crowd by this " draw." Readers of JUSTICE possibly might infer from Vyner's letter that the Social-Democrats of Edinburgh had been frightened into silence by the blatant and egoistic one. Now, as a matter of fact, on the night Vyner speaks of, Malfew Seklew got as unmerciful a drubbing from our comrade Doull, of the Edinburgh branch, as it was ever the fate of an Anarchist to receive at the hands of a class-conscious Socialist. I hope you will insert this and expose an attempt on the part of the Anarchists above mentioned to obtain a cheap advertisement and a further draw.

—Fraternally yours,
Edinburgh. R. R. O'CONNOR.

"We're All More or Less Nutty"

The Kansas City Times   1928

From *The Kansas City Times* (December 28, 1928). Rich details on the talk marathon which included Sirfessor Malfew Seklew can be read in *The Gospel According to Malfew Seklew*. While this article shows our champion in defeat, it nonetheless includes a few golden words not found at any other source.

THE GABBERS MUMBLE ON
A 65-Year-Old Entrant, However,
Quits Because of Drastic Hales.

New York, Dec. 27.—The worlds championship gabfest, at the 71st regiment armory, lost its philosophical mouthpiece today when F. M. Wilkesbarre, Sirfessor of Superology and Lord of Interpretations, Master of Mentoidology and the Demi-god of the Semi-Damned, dropped out of the race.

The 65-year-old founder of the Order of Supercrates, made up of superior human beings numbering 3,000 throughout the world, refused to talk day in and day out unless he could rest while exercising his voice.

"We're all more or less nutty," he said. "Every man in the world is like an iceberg, 80 per cent below the surface; humanity is just a bunch of animated vegetables."

Five had dropped out since the contest began Christmas Day. Six have mumbled and muttered without any rest, save the regular half hour and 45-minute eating periods.

Not Seeking Work

Malfew Seklew

From the *Bradford Weekly Telegraph* (August 3 1906). Almost certainly a previously-undocumented encounter with Sirfessor Malfew Seklew, by way of his public persona F. W. Wilkesbarre.

The following amusing dialogue was over heard on Sunday afternoon at the Bredford unemployed encampment :—

Visitor (addressing one of the leaders): Are you Trade Unionist?

Mr. W– (taken by surprise): Oh, yes.

Visitor: What society do you belong to?

Mr. W–: Oh, I belong to the Society of Social Aristocrats. (Laughter).

Visitor: Looking for work and don't want it. (Renewed laughter).

Mr. W– (boastfully): Oh, yes; quite right. I don't want work. I've lived so long without it, and I'm certain I don't mean to have it now.

Visitor: Well, what are you doing here, then?

Mr. W–: Oh, I'm just helping others to get work, that's all.

Impressed with the leader's candour the visitor went up to him and shook him heartily by the hand.

Seklew Scolds Simpoleons, Supplies Sample Shilling Sericine Silk Set

Malfew Seklew   1914

From *The Daily Herald* (28 March 1914). The egoist superite Sirfessor Malfew Seklew brought his laughing philosophy to two continents in many forms. Sometimes in street oratory, sometimes in books, and sometimes in... novelties.

SIMPOLEONS! Listen! Don't be a blister on the Bosom of Time, but look like Napoleons of Labour by wearing "Sericine" Silk Ties. Something new. Seklew's Sample Shilling Set: 3 Ties, 1 Tie-maker, 1 silver-cased Collar-fastener. 1s the Lot. Agents wanted. Particulars 1d. —Seklew and Co., 11, Chester Street, C.-on-M., Manchester.

No Detail Too Small!
Trevor Blake   **2023**

This small detail from *The Gospel According to Malfew Seklew*, published circa 1927, appeared circa 1916 in *School Sewing Based on Home Problems* by Ida and Myron Burton, published circa 1916. It was a stock illustation element used by printers.

From 1916's *School Sewing Based on Home Problems*:

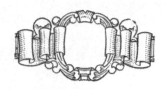

From 1927's *The Gospel According to Malfew Seklew*:

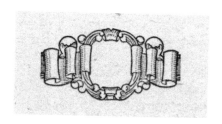

That is all!

RAGNAR REDBEARD

Arthur Desmond was born in New Zealand in 1859. As a young man, working as a station hand, he became a vital force in Antipodian radical politics. He was an advocate of autonomy for the Maori people. In Australia he was a member of the Active Service Brigade, a theosophy-socialist labor union. He wrote and published anonymous and pseudonymous essays and poetry critical of banking and organized religion. He wa arrested and made national news when he vandalized a bank by writing "gone bung" on it (suggesting the bank was about to collapse). When he was subject to arrest for a much more serious crime, he found it expedient to leave the Southern Hemisphere.

Desmond relocated to Chicago, Illinois, where with the exception of a short time in London, he would live the remainder of his days. In 1896 he wrote an expanded version of *Survival of the Fittest* (an essay from his time in Australia) and combined it with *Women and War* and published it as *Might is Right*.

Might is Right was repeatedly reprinted during the author's lifetime. It was wildly popular among radicals and revolutionaries, many of whom lived in Chicago. For a time worked in an ice cream and candy factory.

It was there he met his wife, the mother to his son Arthur Konar Desmond. He sold books through the mail until his death in 1929.

Redbeard in Canada 53
Kevin I. Slaughter   2023

Desmond Selling George 67
Kevin I. Slaughter   2023

Give the New Hand a Show! 75
Kevin I. Slaughter   2023

A.D. in the O.E.D. 81
Kevin I. Slaughter   2023

Introduction to "A Bogus Book" 83
Trevor Blake & Kevin I. Slaughter   2022

A Bogus Book. 84
The Tocsin   1899

Australian Socialist Drinking Club 86
Kevin I. Slaughter   2023

Redbeard's Rough Stuff. 88
C.F. Hunt   1918

"We Understand the Redbeard Philosophy" 90
James Rowan   1918

Voima On Oikeus 92
Covington Hall   1917

No Detail Too Small! 94
Trevor Blake   2023

Redbeard in Canada
Kevin I. Slaughter   2023

In the course of tracing the extensive corpus of poems authored by Arthur Desmond for an upcoming publication, a discernible pattern emerges: his verses have been disseminated widely across both time and geographical boundaries, enduring decades both during his life and posthumously. One of my primary undertakings has involved unearthing the inaugural printings of these poems, scrutinizing their subsequent reprints, and discerning the alterations they underwent in their various iterations. It is well-documented that Desmond exhibited a propensity to appropriate a phrase or an entire poem with minimal modification, firmly affixing his own name to it. In his domain, all verse seemed to be fair game for his appropriation. Furthermore, he did not refrain from self-plagiarism; he would publish the same poem under one pseudonym in a British freethinkers' journal, only to resurface it under a different pseudonym in a Chicago newspaper.

Therefore, when a poem surfaced, attributed to both "Arthur Desmond" and "Gerald Desmond," my initial inclination was to perceive it as an anomaly. However, it unveiled an entirely new chapter in a life shrouded in absolute secrecy for over a century, particularly within this hemisphere. Initially, I harbored suspicions of an inadvertent error or an uncanny coincidence. Yet, with the accumulation of both textual and empirical evidence, my skepticism gradually eroded, leading to an unequivocal acceptance. It transpires that "Ragnar Redbeard" once navigated the sphere of Canadian Socialism!

Evolution

A poem titled "Evolution" was the surprise key to an entire chapter of Arthur Desmond's life that shocked me and has not been documented anywhere else before. I discovered this poem years prior and collected it with every other poem I've gathered up to publish in a third authoritative book of the writing of Arthur Desmond (after *Might is Right: The Authoritative Edition* and *Rival Caesars*). One reason it has taken so long to publish is that I just keep discovering more and more work, but also the work I'd long-discovered reveals it needs a great deal of work and research. Some poems revealed nothing further than themselves, others unveil another writer's pen first wrote the lines, but none have revealed as much as "Evolution".

In the January 20, 1922 issue of *The Socialist* (Melbourne, Victoria, Australia: 1906 - 1923) one could find a poem titled "Evolution" attributed to "Ragnar Redbeard" beneath the title and then after the last line a different attribution: "Arthur Desmond, in 'Western Clarion' Vancouver." This reads very much like an Arthur Desmond poem, but seeing it attributed to a Canadian newspaper was intriguing.

So I followed the thread back in time and discover that in the June 18, 1910 issue of *The International Socialist* (Sydney, NSW, Australia: 1910–1920) one could find a poem titled "Evolution" and attributed to "Gerald Desmond, in *Western Clarion*" Following that thread back in time it is revealed that poem was first published as "A Song of Change" in the April 16, 1910 issue of *Western Clarion* (Vancouver, British Columbia, Canada). A notice in each issue announced the paper was "OWNED AND CONTROLLED BY THE SOCIALIST PARTY OF CANADA".

The two 1910 versions of the poem were printed as follows:

A Song Of Change

Sitting alone by the lake, on the grey cliff's topmost crest;
The voices of night not yet awake, but those of the day at rest;
Musing on Nature's majesty and her mysteries sublime,
I sent my mind thro' obscurity back o'er the eons of time.

Millions of eons ago, ere the day of man had begun,
Before the age of the glacial flow, er the earth was a blazing sun;
A million worlds in embryo, yet nothing there seemed to be,
Save a shimmering, shining, shifting glow like waves of a fiery sea.

A million eons came and past—it seemed in the twink of an
    eye—
Vapor-covered, green and vast a giant Mars whirled by;
I caught a glimpse of bubbling sea, as the vapor upward swirled.
The voice of an earthquake roared at me, and I knew my own
    good world.

Then all was dead, it seemed, and white, and cold, and silent all;
Till a blazing orb flashed on its light and shivered the funeral pall.
I saw the glaciers melt away, the trackless ice-fields pass;
The rocks show out in the light of day, and soon, the green of
    the grass.

Then step by step and age by age, even and night and morn,
I saw the countless battles wage as the many things were born;
Manifold group succeeding group—wondrous forms they were—
Each steadily rising up, fin, scale, feather and fur.

Until at last, and not long ago it seemed in the mists of time
I stood in a forest dark alone, and a creature swung on a vine;
Hairy and wild and brutish he, yet formed on another plan--
The human race in its infancy, neither the ape nor the man.

And next came skin-clad low-browed brutes, yet forms more
        like my own,
Picking the berries and grubbing the roots, chipping the axe of
        stone;
I saw my kind in every age as it learnt to plan and build;
The first rude shed 'gainst nature's rage, the earliest field that
        was tilled.

And as they passed in grand review, the empires one by one,
Quickly they rose before my view, they flourished—and were
        gone.
Step by step and pace by pace, things came and passed away—
I saw the march of the human race from its birth to the present
        day.

I saw this age, the age of gold, of trickery, fraud and force—
But swift the wheels of change now rolled along their onward
        course;
Till I rapturous gazed on a world that was strange, a world from
        slavery free,
And stood amazed at the mighty change and the age of Liberty.

Sitting alone by the lake, by the grey cliff's topmost crest;
The voices of night not yet awake, but those of the day at rest;
Musing on Nature's majesty and' her mysteries sublime,
I sent my mind thru obscurity back o'eer the eons of time.
                    GERALD DESMOND

Evolution

Millions of aeons ago, ere the day of man had begun.
Before the age of the glacial flow, or the earth was a blazing sun;

A million words in embryo, yet nothing there seemed to be,
Save a shimmering, shining, shifting glow like waves on a fiery
    sea.

A million aeons came and past—it seemed in the twink of an
        eye—
Vapor-covered, green and vast, a giant Mars whirled by;
I caught a glimpse of bubbling sea, as the vapor upward swirled,
The voice of an earthquake roared at me, and I knew my own
        good world.

Then all was dead, it seemed, and white and cold, and silent all;
Till a blazing orb flashed on its light, and shivered the funeral
        pall.
I saw the glaciers melt away, the trackless ice-fields pass;
The rocks show out in the light of day, and soon, the green of
        the grass.

Then step by step, and age by age, even and night and morn,
I saw the countless battles wage, as the many things were born;
Manifold group succeeding group—wondrous forms they
        were—
Each steadily rising up, fin, scale, feather, and fur.

Until at last, and not long ago it seemed in the mists of time,
I stood in a forest, dark, alone, and a creature swung on a vine;
Hairy and wild and brutish he, yet formed on another plan—
The human race in its infancy, neither the ape nor the man.

And next came skin-clad, low-browed brutes, yet forms more
        like my own,
Picking the berries and grubbing the roots, chipping the axe of
        stone;
I saw my kind in every age, as it learnt to plan and build;
The first rude shed 'gainst Nature's rage, the earliest field that
        was tilled.

And as they passed in grand review, the empires one by one,
Quickly they rose before my view, they flourished—and were
        gone.
Step by step and pace by pace, things came and passed away—

I saw the march of the human race from its birth to the present
day.

I saw this age, the age of gold, of trickery, fraud and force—
But swift the wheels of change now rolled along their onward
course;
Till I rapturous gazed on a world that was strange, a world from
slavery free,
And stood amazed at the mighty change and the age of Liberty.
—Gerald Desmond, in the *Western Clarion*.

The major difference between the two is the lack of the first and
final repeated stanza. There are only small differences in punctuation
and the word "eons" spelled "aeons" in another. "Eon" is more commonly found in American English, where the other is mostly associated with British English.

The attribution on entry into Australia six months after publication was correct, but after a twelve-year gap, why it was suddenly
attributed to both "Ragnar Redbeard" and "Arthur Desmond," but
still from the correct Canadian paper is puzzling. One thing that may
never be known is why these differences exist, but one cannot deny
they are variations on the same poem, published 12 years apart.

Once the poem was "misattributed", it would be reprinted in
Australian newspapers in 1924, 1927, 1928, 1932, and 1939. Each
of these printings would attribute the poem to "Arthur Desmond
("Ragnar Redbeard")".

An Inconsistent Name in a Limited Sphere

If this "misattribution" of a poem from Gerald to Arthur was a solitary event, and a lone piece of writing, one may excuse it as the mistake of an Australian editor who just assumed the poem was from
the "Desmond he knew" and "fixed the name." But it was not isolated,
and Gerald was anything but a one-hit wonder, and it was not the
only piece of writing that could be confused with Arthur or Ragnar.
So I have to find out everything I can about Gerald.

The Seattle, WA newspaper *The Socialist* of June 22 1907 one
Gerald O'Connell Desmond of Oregon is listed as a "booster" of the
paper. Outside of this, Gerald Desmond seems to exist almost entirely in the world of Canadian Socialists between May 1909 through
December 1911. The 1907 spelling of his middle name is also an

outlier, as otherwise he was referred to as Gerald O'Conel Desmond, G. Desmond, Gerald Desmond, Comrade Desmond, and other variations (but never "G.O.D"). When his middle name is spelled out anywhere other than that one article in 1907, it is always one "n" and one "l". There are lots of ways this inconsistency can be explained away, but in the full context, it makes the most sense that a name changes spelling in such a way because it's not a fixed name.

During that short window of time between 1909 and 1911, Gerald's output was prolific. Gerald Desmond (or some variation of that name) contributed articles, poems and letters to two socialist journals: *Cotton's Weekly* (Montreal) (formerly *The Observer*) and *Western Clarion* (Vancouver). Of the over twenty poems discovered, the titles of a few are "Workers of the World Unite," "A Song of Labor," "Revolution," "Sammy and the Devil," and, remarkably, "Might and Right."

The last poem, published in *Western Clarion* (Vancouver, British Columbia, Canada) Sept. 3, 1910, is as as follows:

Might and Right

Right is might in every time
    So runs the stern grim law;
And every age and every clime
    Has seen the same stern war—
Peoples enslaved and victories won,
From courts upheld by maxim gun
    Back to the fang and claw.

Ethics and creeds have had their day,
    Prophets have come to save;
Ethics and creeds have passed away,
    The prophets find their graves.
Still every race or class of man
Take what they may, hold what they can,
    The weakling still to slave.

So 'tis today as all may see,
    Spite of each lie and fraud.
The veil of sham democracy
    But hides the naked sword.
The slave still writhes beneath the heel,
And rule of right is rule of steel—
    King Plute the overlord.

Slaves of the old time crouched in fright
        Beneath the Tyrant's frown;
They nursed their strength and—might is right—
        Red blazed each stricken town.
They lived or died, it matters naught,
They struck their blow, they had their sport
        They pulled the masters down.

'Tis force, 'tis strength that holdeth ye—
        Thralls of the proletaire—
'Tis force, 'tis power that maketh free—
        Not whine, nor moan, nor prayer,
"Love," "Justice," "Brotherhood"'—forsooth
Might's Right and that's the only truth,
        Strike hard and do not spare.

Our time comes soon, we mark, we learn,
        The hours grow big with fate;
The quickening fires of vengeance burn,
        The white hot flames of hate.
Might's right—the battle's to the strong,
They hold us now, but not for long,
        We gather, watch and wait.
                        GERALD DESMOND.

Someone even only slightly familiar with the writings of Ragnar Redbeard will read not just themes but direct phrases repeated here in a poem that seems a perfect coagulation of the pre-Chicago radical version of Arthur Desmond and the Nietzschean God-stomping Social Darwinist Arthur Desmond.

The poem "Wanderlust" from *Cotton's Weekly* : Vol. XXXVIII, No. 55 (September 30, 1909) mentions Chicago and Australia (along with a lot of other places), but also "The rich plains of Mexico", which is significant because the last chapter of *Rival Caesars* is titled "The Plains of Mexico".

Gerald the Australian Journalist Miner,
Arthur the Australian Journalist Miner

In addition to the great mass of poetry, a few of the more than thirty essays I've cataloged are titled "A Lesson From Australia (For Trades Unionists)," "Socialism and Anarchism," "Free Love and The Home,"

"A Positive Philosophy," "A Few Thoughts About Work."

It is in that first named essay, published in 1909 we can read that Gerald, "while in Australia, became a member of the A.M.A. (Amalgamated Miners of Australia) and worked in the silver-lead mining camp of Broken Hill." While my research had previously turned up *The Daily Telegraph* (Sydney, NSW) reported on April 13, 1894 that

> On Monday night at Wyalong a mass meeting of miners and business people was held on main street. Over 3000 were present. Mr. Arthur Desmond, miner and journalist, was elected chairman. The platform was a 400-gallon tank, on which was placed a kerosene box as a seat for the Chairman.

And in The *Ottawa Journal* (Ottawa, Ontario, Canada) Nov on 27, 1909, we find an article titled "Labor Lecture Against the Navy. It states:

> That standing armies are not essential to the real growth of a country, and that there is no "reason" for the proposed new Canadian navy is the view of Mr. Gerald Desmond, of the Western Federation of Miners, who is in the city for a few days and will speak at the Nickel theatre here twice tomorrow.
>
> He has been connected with the labor movement officially for the past fourteen years in the United States, in Australia and New Zealand, and to some extent Canada.

The Western Federation of Miners is the organization that Bill Haywood was associated with, along with Jack Jones of the Dil Pickle Club, before they helped found the Industrial Workers of the World. Importantly, We know Arthur emigrated to Chicago in 1896, which would be roughly the same "fourteen years" before the article was written.

But the most important newspaper article was titled "Socialist Speakers" and appeared in *The Ottawa Citizen* (Ottawa, Ontario, Canada) Nov 24, 1909, the second sentence starts the important section:

> The Nickel theater will probably be engaged, for the occasion and large attendances are expected as both speakers are well

known men. Mr. Desmond, who hails from Australia, has the distinction of having edited the first labor paper there. It was 40 years ago. At the time of the great labor troubles in Australia he was imprisoned for nine months for his part in them. Later he came to America and now holds office in the Western Federation of Miners. "I have been nineteen times in prison," says Mr. Desmond, "and I may be in again." He has had some municipal experience," having twice run as a candidate In his home municipality In Australia. He was once elected but disqualified on account of not coming under the regulations as regards citizenship, etc.

If we scale back the claims a bit to allow for gross hyperbole (a trait of Arthur Desmond), at its heart is that Gerald was a radical newspaper publisher in Australia, had many run-ins with the law and ran for office twice. All these things track exactly to the life of Arthur Desmond.

A Second Canadian Pseudonym

As fascinating, shocking and amusing as the discovery of "Redbeard in Canada" was, the revelations kept coming. I was awestruck when a second pseudonym pops up upon the discovery of darker letters and poems signed off as "HIBERNICUS", a name that means "pertaining to the Irish." One stand out is that while others discuss meeting Gerald in person, and meeting notes refer to his presence, there are no such letters about Hibernicus, even though he writes about speaking in public and being in different locations, and meeting with people.

When compiling a master list of Gerald's materials, I noticed an article titled "'Mad' Philosophy" which contained quotes attributed to Friedrich Nietzsche in the June 24, 1911 issue of *Western Clarion*, next to an article signed "Desmond" about "a new system of production... forced on a backward country and people." I immediately compared the quotes to *The Sayings of Nietzsche*, published by a different Arthur Desmond pseudonym. While none of the quotes matched, two things stood out to me: the tenor of the quotes ("The master has as much law or right over his slave as his power extends" is a standout), and also the fact that many of the quotes can't be found in the existing English translations of Nietzsche, which is similar to "Sayings of Nietzsche" and a classic trademark of Arthur Desmond to rewrite or fabricate material at will.

One of the clinchers for me were two letters, in columns

side-by-side in the June 10, 1911 issue. The first was a very short and simple letter from Desmond, updating his comrades about his goings on. "Since last report have been doing mostly street and literature propaganda... am now resting a sore throat for a few days." And in the next column we read about Hibernicus having dinner with a family in Kootenays, where he was called to talk. The comrade's wife had made a meal for them all and when all were seated the comrade "raised his hand and hung down his head". A prayer before dinner was enough to set the hungry man off his meal:

> Here is a wage-slave—working 10 hours per day, and hard work at that, with a daily wage of $2.75 to keep self and family on... getting... less than one-fifth of the value of his labor. Fancy such a one being thankful! To me the very thought of thing is sickening. Next night I pit up a spiel on the street–dealing with "Slave Religions." Some of the bunch wondered what made me so bitter. I answered them in the language of science, that every effect has a cause.

Struggle for Existence, Survival of the Fittest and the Disappearance of Comrade Desmond

In 1911 16-page booklet written by Desmond was published by the Socialist Party of Canada titled *The Struggle for Existence*. The contents are, to my frustration, rather bland socialist pablum, but I am baffled that the title for Gerald's first book is nearly identical to Desmond's first book.

It was at the end of the same year that reports began to be published:

> (Meeting Nov. 6 1911) Evidence being presented showing extreme irregularity of conduct on the part of Gerald Desmond, committee decided to warn all locals against entrusting this man with any funds of, or the performance of any duty for, the party.
>
> (NOVEMBER 18, 1911)

> Some parties in the Boundary district will notice that their contributions are absent from this account of receipts. This is due to the fact that the collector, Gerald Desmond, did not give me any account of these contributions, nor did he remit any money to me...
>
> (DECEMBER 18, 1911)

WORKERS OF THE WORLD UNITE

The WESTERN CLARION

PUBLISHED IN THE INTERESTS OF THE WORKING CLASS ALONE

NO. 17.

Vancouver, British Columbia, Saturday, June 24, 1911.

Subscription Price
Per Year $1.00

THE ONLY CURE

The Present System of Property Must Give Place to Collective Ownership.

NECESSITY.

"MAD" PHILOSOPHY

ANOTHER IN LINE

Backward Country Brought Up-to-Date in the Interests of Bourgeois Business.

IN LIGHTER VEIN.

THE NEW EMPIRE.
By Bill Gee

—HIBERNICUS.

"MAD" PHILOSOPHY

(The Philosophy of Nietzsche is often overlooked by revolutionists. While the so-called "mad philosopher" cannot be taken seriously at all times, still his writings abound with phrases and sentences which might often be utilized. He was a believer in evolution and a determined opponent of the metaphyshic school.)

"It is the characteristic of an advanced civilization to set a higher value upon little simple things, ascertained by scientific methods, than upon the pleasing and magnificent errors originating in metaphysical epochs and people.'

This is good. The painstaking scientist at least does add something, however small, to human knowledge. The metaphysician simply wanders round in the maze of introspective speculation—and gets nowhere.

"Any seriousness in symbolism is the indication of a deficient education."

"Inasmuch as all metaphysic has concerned itself with freedom of the will, it should be designated as the science that deals with fundamental errors as if they were fundamental truths."

"The good (powerful) are a caste, the bad (weak) are a quantity like dust. GOOD AND BAD IS TANTAMOUNT TO NOBLE AND SERVILE, MASTER AND SLAVE."

"Our existing morality has developed upon the foundation laid by ruling races and castes."

"Religions are very rich in refuges from the mandate of suicide, therefore, they ingratiate themselves with those who cling to life."

"THE MASTER HAS AS MUCH LAW OR RIGHT OVER HIS SLAVE AS HIS POWER EXTENDS."

"Everything uttered by the ordinary philosopher on the subject of man is, in the last resort, nothing more than a piece of testimony concerning man during a limited period. Lack of the historical sense is the traditional defect of all common philosophers."

"Many essential things in human evolution took place aeons ago, long before the four thousands years or so of which history tells us."

"Everything evolved. THERE ARE NO ETERNAL FACTS, AS THERE ARE NO ABSOLUTE TRUTHS."

"Astrology pre-supposes that the heavenly bodies are regulated in their movements by the destiny of mortals. So the moral man supposes that that which concerns himself must also be the heart of things."

"When a murderer is executed the guilt, if there be any, is not punished. This guilt is really ascribable to the teachers, the parents, the ENVIRONMENT and the pre-disposing circumstances generally.'

"We must always remember that man has evolved—that the intellectual faculty itself is an evolution, whereas some philosophers make the whole cosmos out of this intellectual faculty."

"All common philosophers make the mistake of taking contemporary man as THEIR STARTING POINT and trying through an analysis of him to reach a final canclusion."

"Even were the existence of a metaphysical world established it would nevertheless remain true that OF ALL KINDS OF KNOWLEDGE, KNOWLEDGE OF SUCH A WORLD WOULD BE OF THE LEAST CONSEQUENCE —of even less consequence than the knowledge of the chemical composition of water to a storm-tossed mariner."

(There is much more good stuff in the Nietzschen philosophy, but the above are fair examples. Neitzsche never truly or completely sensed the importance of the economic factor in life (though he saw it dimly), but at least he repudiated and attacked the metaphysic and riddled theology full of holes.)

—HIBERNICUS.

Gerald Desmond was not a mere name on paper. He toured on behalf of the Canadian Socialists and they raised money for him and he sold books. And eventually, after the discovery of "extreme irregularity" in Gerald's accounting, he was gone with the wind.

Arthur Desmond is Gerald Desmond

In print, over the course of a small handful of years, Gerald Desmond recounted narratives of his daily life as a Canadian Socialist stump speaker and organizer. However, there is no evidence of *this* Gerald Desmond before or after this specific temporal window. In December of 1911, a notice indicating Desmond's failure to submit either a report of received funds or any remittances constituted the final mention of him in the news. The subsequent year bore only two passing references to him, both in the past tense, signifying his complete disappearance as an active activist or writer. The same time that Gerald disappeared, so did Hibernicus.

It is crucial to underscore that Arthur Desmond meticulously self-obscured his identity in America, achieving such an effective concealment that only in the mid-1980s did British egoist anarchist Sidney E. Parker, a historian specializing in individualist and egoist figures influenced by Max Stirner, definitively link Arthur Desmond to Ragnar Redbeard. Even then, it was not until the last decade, approximately one hundred and twenty years after his arrival on the shores of his ultimate adopted homeland, that this association gained acknowledgment and dissemination among independent researchers. During the years Gerald Desmond was touring Canada, there was hardly any trace of Arthur's activities in the United States, and when we have record of activity in 1911, it signals the beginning of a revival of activity after a seemingly long-dormant period.

In the course of my research, the initial evidence suggesting that Arthur Desmond and Gerald Desmond were one and the same initially appeared to be a potential error or perhaps a fortuitous coincidence. As I amassed further evidence, the weight of it grew to the point where I began to entertain the notion that it might be too good to be true, possibly tainted by confirmation bias. While I harbored deep skepticism, I remained vigilant against allowing my enthusiasm for uncovering new facets of this intriguing figure, on whom I have expended a substantial amount of time, to unduly influence my judgment. Eventually, the accumulation of numerous anecdotes, consistent timelines, and textual and thematic correlations compelled me to accept the seemingly whimsical premise that his primary obfuscation was to just change his first name. This occurred during the period when he fervently championed a form of "superman socialism" intrinsically linked to motifs of strength and assertiveness, which have remained defining features of his life's work.

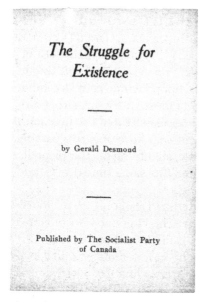

↑ Title page for *The Struggle for Existence* by Gerald Desmond (Vancouver: The Socialist Party of Canada, 1911).

↑ Title page for *Borot'ba za istnovanie* (The Struggle for Existence) by Gerald Desmond (Vancouver: Nakladom "Pravdy i voli", 1920). Ukranian translation.

DESMOND SELLING GEORGE

Kevin I. Slaughter   2023

Notices in New Zealand Newspapers link the author of *Might is Right* to Henry George. These notices are proletarian sales-pitches for Geroge's late-19th century hit *Progress and Poverty*. His ideas launched a sort of "third party" alternative to capitalism and socialism that appealed to the "radicals" of the time. Desmond would quote from the book, including using the phrase "Land and Liberty" during his 1884 parliamentary run. Desmond would later refer to George as a "seductive but most malignant State Socialist" in *Might is Right*.

∉

This notice appeared in the *Hawke's Bay Herald* on the 12th, 16th, and 17th of November in 1885, and in the *Poverty Bay Independent* on November 24, 1885:

> Muddy-brained drudges! White-wage slaves
> Multitudinous asses! Light, more light!
> —CARLYLE.
>
> ## TO THE PEOPLE OF HAWKE'S BAY.
>
> ALL Intelligent Working-men should carefully read "Progress and Poverty," by Henry George, that they may thoroughly comprehend the horrid grind of their slavish position, and the REAL cause of social misery and hard times. Read and remember that "Knowledge is power." Because you have been gulled and robbed in the past, that is no reason why you should, like cowardly cringing curs, literally lie down to be both spurned and robbed NOW.
> ARTHUR DESMOND.
> Hastings, November, 1885.
>
> *Price 1s, from any Bookseller.* 789

The notice begins with a quote:

"Muddy-brained drudges! White-wage slaves Multitudinous! Light, more light!" and is atributed to "Carlyle".

I have found no source for this quote. Desmond was a life-long prevaricator, but this fabrication appears particularly bold.

However, It is commonly repeated that Goethe's last words were "Light! More light!"

The phrase "knowledge is power" is often attributed to Francis Bacon, from his *Meditationes Sacrae* (1597). Thomas Jefferson used the phrase in his correspondence on at least four occasions in the early 1800s, each time in connection with the establishment of a state university in Virginia.

The alliteration of "cowardly cringing curs" is unusual for Desmond, so it was not a surprise to find the exact phrase in *The Melbourne Riots and how Harry Holdfast and his Friends Emancipated the Workers* (1892) by David Alfred Andrade:

> If you enslave me, I learn to rejoice in slavery. If you treat me brutally, you encourage brutality in my nature, and I act brutally to you. If in this land, which naturally belongs to all you who live upon it, you give me a special privilege to the ownership of this land, you make me a tyrant, and I cannot help but act like a tyrant; and you make yourselves my serfs and cowardly cringing curs willing to lick my feet in truly slave-like fashion, that I may graciously afford you permit to toil on the land I have deprived you of.

In May 1886, Andrade and a group of individuals established the Melbourne Anarchist Club. Andrade was associated with Australian radicals like S.A. Rosa and J.A. Andrews. Desmond joined this circle after departing from New Zealand, although he didn't reach Australia until approximately 1893. The repetition of the phrase "cowardly cringing curs" initially led me to speculate that there might have been some form of communication between Desmond and the Australian radicals prior to his arrival.

Possibly the phrase was coincidental, or maybe it was phrase of Desmond's coinage that he would influence others to use.

What is an issue is apparent: *The Melbourne Riots* was published seven years *after* Desmond placed the notice in a newspaper. I was able to find the *shorter* phrase "cringing curs" in the popular Australian journal *The Bulletin* in 1887 (two years too late) and many later references, but never the full three word phrase. The solitary use of the phrase predating Desmond's, was in the sentence "Away with such paltry, cowardly, cringing curs!" But that was published in *The Democrat-Star* published out of Pascagoula, Mississippi on

September 19, 1879. An unlikely source!

This became even more likely when I stumbled across the phrase in one more place: *Official Proceedings of the Fifteenth Annual Convention of the Western Federation of Miners* from 1907. On the Seventeenth Day, June 28, 2907, at the Odd Fellows Hall of Denver, Colorado.

The convention was called to order by Chairman William Davidson and a handful of delagate speakers commented on the topic of the day. J.F. Hutchinson, Robert Randall, J.W. Scott, Mike Tonrey, R.M. Rodger, Teofila Petriella, Vincent St. John, and others.

After a bit of cacophany, J.F. Hutchinson was able to command the floor and addressed the convention regarding the contoversy surrounding the connection of the WFM and the Industrial Workers of the World (after IWW). The IWW were attempting to take over the WFM, and the WFM were trying to sever associations.

> "...if you for a quarter of a second secede from the IWW, I want to tell you my opinion of you will be that you are a bunch of cowardly, cringing curs."

The IWW was launched in Chicago just two years prior by 200 socialists, anarchists, Marxists, and radical trade unionists. The idea was to create "one big union" and fight for all workers instead of having unions based on trades. It was, in part, a reaction to the dominance of the American Federation of Labor. The IWW's founders included William D. ("Big Bill") Haywood, James Connolly, Daniel De Leon, Eugene V. Debs, Thomas Hagerty, Lucy Parsons, Mary Harris "Mother" Jones, Frank Bohn, William Trautmann, Vincent Saint John, Ralph Chaplin.

Most of these names can be connected to Ragnar Redbeard and his infamous book *Might is Right*, either directly or by one or two removes. *Might is Right* was considered to be the "Bible of the IWW" by numerous contemporary writers, and has been well documented in "Ragnar Redbeard and the Industrial Workers of the World" by Trevor Blake, found in *Der Geist,* Issue 3 (Spring 2020).

Vincent St. John was of the Chicago IWW group, and it is clear that Hutchinson was aligned with the IWW as well. While there is no direct proof that Hutchinson and Desmond had ever communicated, they were both comrades with many of the same people, and haunted the same Chicago locales.

Three uses of the alliterative curse documented in three different countries over the course of two decades, first by Desmond and then by people that he either knew or is known to have been in the same milieu with.

∉

In the *Poverty Bay Independent* of January 26, 1886, the following article appeared:

Henry George's Works.

For some time past a fervent appeal "To the People" has been appearing regularly in the *Napier Evening News*, emanating from Mr. A. Desmond, a late Greyite candidate for the representation of Hawke's Bay County. It is to the following effect:—

[The blinded sire slaves himself out and leaves a blinded son, and men made in the image of God continue as mere two-legged, broken-spirited, beasts of burden.]
—THOMAS CARLYLE.

EVERY truly thoughtful elector should seriously prepare for the coming struggle. Mr. Gladstone tersely and truly says:— "The people do not know what they want, if they did they might demand it with success." To know your want read "Social Problems," by Henry George (Price 1s from any Bookseller, 1s 8d Posted) It is high time you began to think— to act like men in grim earnest. Your destiny is in your own hands, and in the sublime worlds of old "Behold ye shall grow wiser or ye shall die." Be not longer, in the language of your owners, "Splendidly Stupid." —ARTHUR DESMOND.

The power of a well circulated popular book has in all social movements been immense. The role which Rousseau played to the French Revolution, one hundred years ago, by the publication of his "Contract Sociale," is now being adopted by Mr. Henry George in the publication and worldwide circulation of his two celebrated works—"Progress and Poverty" and "Social Problems."

The "Contract Sociale" precipitated in France (not without bloodshed), one of the greatest reforms in modern times. Let us hope that if "Progress and Poverty" has a similar effect upon English speaking communities, that the reform will be fought upon constitutional principles, and not, as in Paris, by means of street barricades, whiffs of grape shot and the guillotine.

A suggestive anecdote is related of the late Thomas Carlyle, the great Philosopher and Historian. He was once discussing, in a miscellaneous company, the merits of a popular orator, when an aristocratic fop said; "He was all theory—mere theory." Carlyle replied in his characteristic manner:— "Once upon a time a young man came to Paris and wrote a book; feather heads and aristocrats sneered and laughed at it as 'mere theory,' but the second edition was bound in their skins."

Much as we object to our Colonial money lending, and land owning aristocracy, still we have no wish to see an edition of "Progress and Poverty" "bound in their skins." Still it is hard to say what might happen if an angry people took the hint. Meanwhile the people should read the book.

It is to the detriment of my research that the *Napier Evening News* has not been digitised, and I cannot yet discover if there is more of Desmond's writing there.

The quote attributed to "Mr. Gladstone" could not be sourced, but it was certainly British politician William Ewart Gladstone, of the Liberal Party, that he was referencing. Gladstone would hold many offices, including Prime Minister many times. In 1886 he proposed "home rule" for Ireland, and Desmond, of Irish extraction, was very involved in what was known as "the Irish question". It is possible he is paraphrasing a quotation, or fabricating one entirely.

The quotation that begins "The blinded sire..." is from Carlyle's *Chartism*. The unattributed quote that begins "Behold ye shall..." is from Carlyle's *Past & Present* Book 1, Chapter 5. Desmond quotes himself in another short bit of alliteration with the phrase "spendidly stupid."

Note that Desmond here is publicly hoping that the "liberal position" (i.e. the peaceful spread ideas given in George) gains the "might" to become right, rather than the bloodshed of revolution.

¢

The following notice appeared in the *Daily Telegraph* four months later on March 12, 1886:

Similarly to the previous items, it begins with a quote attributed to Thomas Carlyle. Here is a truncated version of the story told in the January 26th notice:

"Once upon a time a young man came to Paris and wrote a book. Fops, aristocrats, and fools laughed and sneered at it as 'theory, mere theory,' but the next edition was bound in their skins."

It appears this quote comes to us only second-hand, via *Doctor Claudius: A True Story* by F. Marion Crawford (London; Macmillan And Co., 1883). The larger context of the quote is from Chapter 14:

Thomas Carlyle, late of Chelsea, knew that. How he hit and hammered and churned in his wrath, with his great cast-iron words. How the world shrieked when he wound his tenacious fingers in the glory of her golden hair and twisted and wrenched and twisted till she yelled for mercy, promising to be good, like a whipped child. There is a story told of him which might be true.

It was at a dinner-party, and Carlyle sat silent, listening to the talk of lesser men, the snow on his hair and the fire in his amber eyes. A young Liberal was talking theory to a beefy old Conservative, who despised youth and reason in an equal degree.

"The British people, sir," said he of the beef, "can afford to laugh at theories."

"Sir," said Carlyle, speaking for the first time during dinner, "the French nobility of a hundred years ago said they could afford to laugh at theories. Then came a man and wrote a book called the *Social Contract*. The man was called Jean-Jacques Rousseau, and his book was a theory, and nothing but a theory. The nobles could laugh at his theory; *but their skins went to bind the second edition of his book*[1]."

[1]   There was a tannery of human skins at Meudon during the Revolution.

This story has been repeated in newspaper and books since, but it doesn't seem as if it were ever confirmed as anything more than heresay.

The rest of the notice is familiar in tone to Desmond, and later Redbeard, though Redbeard might not suggest that one spend time "demanding justice for his fellow man."

In *Might is Right: The Authoritative Edition* (AMiR 2.7:2) we read Desmond writing as Redbeard:

> Another seductive but most malignant State Socialist (Henry George) roundly proclaims that "The salvation of society, the hope of the free and full development of humanity is in the gospel of brotherhood, the gospel of Christ," and thereupon he proposes to make politicians the national rent-tax collectors, administrators of everything in general, and all-round Distributors of State Pensions to "the poor and needy." Has not mankind had sufficient experience of what politicians are?—Those black-hearted creeping thieves and frauds. Their sting is deadlier than the bite of a cobra, and in the breath of their mouth there is—DEATH. Curses be upon you, O ye politicians, and upon all who advocate increasing your prerogatives!

Here Desmond quotes from page 20 of Henry George's *Social Problems* (Chicago, 1883).

The larger context of that quote shows Desmond has not taken the quotation out of context or altered it significantly:

In a "journal of civilization" a professed teacher declares the saving word for society to be that each shall mind his own business. This is the gospel of selfishness, soothing as soft flutes to those who, having fared well themselves, think everybody should be satisfied. But the salvation of society, the hope for the free, full development of humanity, is in the gospel of brotherhood — the gospel of Christ. Social progress makes the well-being of all more and more the business of each ; it binds all closer and closer together in bonds from which none can escape. He who observes the law and the proprieties, and cares for his family, yet takes no interest in the general weal, and gives no thought to those who are trodden under foot, save now and then to bestow alms, is not a true Christian. Nor is he a good citizen. The duty of the citizen is more and harder than this.

The type of full reverse from such enthusiastic advocation of Henry George and his work, to condemning him in such vociferous terms, has made many readers presume that *Might is Right* is a work of satire.

Give the New Hand a Show!
Kevin I. Slaughter

ELECTORS OF HAWKE'S BAY COUNTY!

MESSRS.

SUTTON & RUSSELL

HAVE

MISREPRESENTED YOU

FOR ABOUT TEN YEARS!

WHAT HAVE THEY DONE FOR YOU?

Nothing but increasing taxation for you and making the battle of life harder. They have been weighed in the balance and found wanting.

GIVE THE NEW HAND A SHOW!

VOTE FOR DESMOND!

Vote for the Liberal Party!

VOTE FOR LAND AND LIBERTY!

AND

"IN THIS SIGN SHALL YE CONQUER."

se of you desirous of avenging Captain Russell's treatment of Mr. Sutton should vote for DESMOND and keep the "Captain" out.

This remarkable electoral poster and the folowing political cartoon have been two of my most exciting graphic discoveries in researching the life and word of Arthur "Ragnar Redbeard" Desmond.

Arthur Desmond was active in radical politics in New Zealand in the late 1800s and attempted to run for Parliament as a candidate for Hawke's Bay twice. Heavily influenced by Henry George's book *Progress and Poverty*, he was a regular letter writer to the *New Zealand Times* in the years leading up to his candidacy.

∉

In September of 1883 Desmond used the first pseudonym of dozens he would use over his lifetime. He reveals himself when he says the same things under his own name as he does using assumed names. For example, this excerpt from a letter to the editor of the *Hawke's Bay Herald*:

> Even now in old bottles the new wine begins to ferment and elemental forces gather for the strife—the strife in which right shall conquer might. Then let our motto for the onset be "Land and Liberty," In hoc signo vinces.
> — I am, &c,
> Te Tua.

These few lines are a skeleton key to unlocking secrets of a lifetime that follow. He establishes two phrases he would closely associated himself with. The first, *In Hoc Signo Vinces,* translates to "in this sign you shall conquer", and was the vision of Constantine to give divine support to his warfare. The slogan "Land and Liberty" had, as previously detailed in the essay "Desmond Selling George", entered the vernacular of radical politics via the Russian Nihilists.[1] While these all are references to things that exist in the world, more importantly both phrases[2] reside in *Progress and Poverty*, including the phrase:

> "Even now, in old bottles the new wine begins to ferment, and elemental forces gather for the strife!"

---

1   *Progress and Poverty*, Book 6, Chapter 5: "The ideal of socialism is grand and noble; and it is, I am convinced, possible of realization; but such a state of society cannot be manufactured—it must grow. Society is an organism, not a machine. It can live only by the individual life of its parts. And in the free and natural development of all the parts will be secured the harmony of the whole. All that is necessary to social regeneration is included in the motto of those Russian patriots sometimes called Nihilists—'Land and Liberty!'"

2   Chapter 5 of Henry George's 1881 work "The Irish Land Question" is titled "In Hoc Signo Vinces"

Ragnar Redbeard

So, possibly most important of all, we find Desmond lifting text from another source without attribution. Desmond would be involved in a national plagiarism scandal over his poem "Christ as Social Reformer," and *Might is Right: The Authoritative Edition* details his prolific use of uncredited materials. There are many terms we can use for Arthur Desmond's writing, two unkind but true terms are "prevaricator" and "plagiarist".

Finally, I will draw the reader's attention to the line added to the end of George's biblical allusion: "right shall conquer might". This author would one day completely invert this into a phillipic of mastery, right cannot conquer might, because right is derived from it. This reversal is first announced to the world under the name of "Mr. Smith", speaking in the basement of a Christian Charity house in Chicago a decade later.[3]

A July 5th, 1884 notice, signed A. Desmond, began "To the Electors of Hawke's Bay County." It announced that Desmond had "decided to become a Candidate for your suffrages." The announcement finished "A Land Tax and No Land Monopoly shall be my motto, and my aim to settle Human Beings upon our lands instead of Sheep."

The full-page advertisement in the July 25th, 1884 issue of *Hawke's Bay Herald*, presented at the head of this article, begins the same "THE ELECTORS OF HAWKES BAY COUNTY!"

This poster is unique in that it is the only known campaign item for Desmond's political career that was not just a plain notice published in newspapers. While this was printed in a newspaper, it was a whole page set in special type, unlike all other known notices.

The next few lines read "MSSRS. SUTTON AND RUSSEL HAVE MISREPRESENTED YOU FOR ABOUT TEN YEARS! WHAT HAVE THEY DONE FOR YOU? Nothing but increasing taxation for you and making the battle of life harder. They have been weighed in the balance and found wanting."

Frederick Sutton and Sir William Russell were Desmon's opponents in the election, and both were well known figures in local politics. Sutton was a settle, shopkeeper and farmer. He was the incumbent, having won his seat in 1881, after having served two terms as a representative for Napier. Russell was in politics from 1870 to

---

3   See "'The Philosophy Of Power,' A Previously Unknown Speech by Ragnar Redbeard" in *Der Geist* Issue 4.

1905. He was a major land owner and had the reputation of serving the interests of other land owners against the interest of the working man. He would eventually become recognized as the Leader of the Opposition emergent, then known as the Conservative Party.

The next line announced "GIVE THE NEW HAND A SHOW!". Desmond is known to have worked as a "station hand" as early as 1878, when he worked as a laborer (i.e. "hand") on the sheep farm (known as a "station" in Australia and New Zealand) known as Wingate Station, owned by John Wingate. The station was located nearer the south east of the north island. desmond was exhorting the eloctorates to show up at the polls to vote for him. The editor of the *Hawke's Bay Herald* wrote, elsewhere, "We only know that Mr. Desmond is a cattle-drover, and that he is of Radical tendencies."

The next four lines are all very fascinating. "VOTE FOR DESMOND!" clearly announces the name of Arthur Desmond. "Vote for the Liberal Party!" is a fascinating line, as the Liberal Party did not yet *formally* exist in 1884, meaning Desmond was one of the earliest candidates to run on the platform that would develop into the first political party of New Zealand, which was elected into power in 1891. Within two years they extended suffrage to women, the first country in the world to have "universal suffrage".[4] Elsewhere it is documented that many of Desmond's compatriots in New Zealand and Australia would become national leaders.

"Vote For Land and Liberty!" is a reference to his Georgist ideals, detailed previously, but also the Russian secret society that first appeared in the early 1860s, named *Zemlya i volya* (Land and Liberty) issuing propaganda under that name advocating a peasant revolution. After political oppression it disbanded after a few years of activity until reformation in the late 1870s as a populist movement.

The second catch-phrase Desmond would use through his life is presented "In This Sign Ye Shall Conquer," whose meaning as also already detailed. But much like many of the positions he would take as a younger man, he inverted them by the time he arrived to America.

---

4   The mind is both fascinated and surprised by the direct, positive, and literal connection between "Ragnar Redbeard" and the political movement that brought about women's suffrage globally. Contemporary academics and journalists cast a shadow on their profession when they oversimplify him, dismissing him as inconsequential or using him as a tool for persecution. Their actions represent a grave form of propaganda and, more importantly, oversimplify a multifaceted individual into a one-dimensional target for their prejudice and narrow-mindedness.

Ragnar Redbeard

The following illustration reveals perfectly this inversion, appearing in one of Desmond's Chicago journals titled *The Lion's Paw: A Journal of the Gods*, numbered Vol. 7 No. 3, and dated March 1913.

The image of a priest with a raised cross is given the legend "iN THiS SIGN YOU ARE CONQUERED", putting the reader in the role of potential victim of the priest, rather than comrade.

The poster is completed with a statement about the ncessity for a change in political leadership. It is unclear what Mr. Russell did to Mr. Sutton that Desmond and his votors would be avenging.

¢

The illustration "The New hand culling the flock" is an unsigned 1884 political cartoon featuring Arthur Desmond (1859–1929) as a stockman flexing his "Land Tax" whip while riding his horse "Liberal Party." The July 21st 1884 issue of *The Daily Telegraph* noted:

> The present election contest has been enlivened by the issue of numerous illustrated skits, cleverly designed and capitally drawn... A very good one is entitled "The new hand culling the flock," in which Mr. Desmond is driving Messrs Tanner, Ormond, Sutton, and Russell, who are represented by sheep. The style in which these skits have been turned out reflects much credit on the lithographer.

The New Hand culling the flock.

The sheep in the illustration represented Thomas Tanner, Frederick Sutton, William Russell, and John Ormond, who were all running for Parliament in the area.

The sheepdog labeled "Sr. G.G." represents Sir George Grey, whom Desmond looked up to, and who ran unopposed in Auckland East that year. The sheepdog labeled "W.H." is most likely William John Hurst who represented the Waitemata electorate.

The caption to the illustration is inspired by one of the slogans Desmond used, referring to himself as the "New Hand."

There are only a handful of illustrations of Desmond, some documented in Previous issues of *Der Geist*. The one thing that is unclear is if the example is the finished illustration, or a sketch. It is a bit hurried in appearance.

Desmond lost to William Russell by a large number of votes in that 1883 election, though he lost by a much smaller margin in a second run three years later. Those were the only known attempts at a legitimage political career. It would be radical publisher and propagandist for the rest of his life.

A.D. in the O.E.D.

Kevin I. Slaughter   2023

> **bung,** *a.*² *Austral.* and *N.Z. slang.* Also
> formerly bong. [*Austral.* Aboriginal word.]
>   **a.** Dead. **b.** Bankrupt. **c.** Ruined, useless. Also
> in phr. *to go bung*, to die; to fail; to go bankrupt.
>   [1847 J. D. LANG *Cooksland* x. 430 A place called *Umpie
> Bung*, or the dead houses.] 1882 W. A. J. BOYD *Old Colonials*
> 73 Just afore you hands 'im [*sc.* the horse] over and gets the
> money, he goes bong on you [i.e. he dies]. 1885 *Austral.
> Printers' Keepsake* 40 His musical talent had 'gone bung'.
> 1885 H. FINCH-HATTON *Adv. Australia* x. 142 Directly me
> bung (die) me jump up white feller. 1893 *Argus* 15 Apr. 13/2
> (Morris), All flesh is grass, says the preacher, . . And we gaze
> on a bank in the evening, and lo, in the morn 'tis bung. **1893**
> *Melbourne Herald* 25 Apr. 2/4 (Morris), One member of the
> mischief-making brotherhood wrote the words 'gone bung'
> under a notice on the Government Savings Bank. 1902 W.
> SATCHELL *Land of Lost* vii. 47 The merchant princes who
> have gone bung, and the geniuses who have gone bunger.
> 1930 A. GROOM *Merry Christmas* xxvi. 209 The telephone
> line's been mostly bung and broke since, but I got through.
> 1948 L. MACFARLANE *This N.Z.* xiv. 137 We were bung,
> completely down and out. 1952 G. WILSON *Julien Ware* viii.
> 68 'Why aren't you playing?'.. 'Got a bung ankle. Don't
> want to hurt it again.'

While in Australia, Arthur Desmond published the journal *Hard Cash* where he took to task bankers, the lords of industry, and the church. His journal was seen as such a threat to the economy, booksellers and news dealer who sold the paper were rounded up and persecuted.

There was a general panic about the stability of the dollar, and while his journal was feared and caused its own ripples, it was just a two word bit of grafitti that was able to capture the attentions of the national press.

The Australian journal *The Bulletin* of May 13, 1983 reported:

> Arthur Desmond, who was fined £3 and costs in Sydney the other day for writing the words, " gone bung," on the Government notice guaranteeing the re-payment of the money lodged by depositors in the N.S.W. Savings Bank, strongly contends that he performed a public-service in drawing attention to the insecure condition of the deposits aforesaid failing a permanent Government guarantee—inasmuch as at least the liquid portion of the savings of the public are deposited in one or other of the associated banks. When Desmond was arrested, the police and the press gave it out that he was insane.

Edward Ellis Morris' *Austral English: A Dictionary of Australasian Words, Phrases and Usages* (London, Macmillan and Co.: 1898), had a reference of note for "Bung".

> **1893.** 'The Herald' (Melbourne), April 25, p. 2, col. 4:
> "Perhaps Sydney may supply us with a useful example. One member of the mischief-making brotherhood wrote the words `gone bung' under a notice on the Government Savings Bank, and he was brought before the Police Court charged with damaging the bank's property to the extent of 3*d*. The offender offered the Bench his views on the bank, but the magistrates bluntly told him his conduct was disgraceful, and fined him £3 with costs, or two months' imprisonment."

A shortened version of that reference was later culled for one of the many definitions of "bung" found on page 657 of the second Volume of *The Oxford English Dictionary*, Second Edition, as presented at the head of this article.

Thus it was that Arthur "Ragnar Redbeard" Desmond found his way into "the greatest publishing event of the century" when the second edition of that dictionary was published.

Introduction to "A Bogus Book"
Trevor Blake & Kevin I. Slaughter   2022

The letter presented here as "A Bogus Book" is from *The Tocsin*, March 23, 1899. Reviews of Ragnar Redbeard's book vary in the extreme from the beginning. Arthur Desmond, who wrote as Ragnar Redbeard, first shows up in New Zealand in the early 1880s.

Desmond was a prolific poet and agitator, had his work published in numerous newspapers, editing a number of his own journals, and causing multiple national scandals. He was a high profile radical until he fled to the United States and settled in Chicago in 1896.

His most famous work had two different titles and multiple subtitles. The first issuance circa 1896 was under the title *The Survival of the Fittest*, followed the next year by a fully fleshed out *Might is Right*. Multiple sources state he began work on it while still in Australia.

While many of his comrades in Australia knew Desmond was Redbeard, in America he was able to keep his authorship more or less veiled in secrecy for a century. If *The Tocsin* knew Redbeard's real identity, they didn't tip their hand to it.

The *Tocsin* was a radical socialist journal that was edited, for a time, by Desmond's eccentric anarchist compatriot John Arthur Andrews. Andrews edited the journal for a few months before his health failed, but between May and July 1900 he published a series of recollections titled "On Active Service: Items in the History of the People's Movement in Australia." Those writings, that mention Desmond, have been collected and published as an issue of *Stand Alone* (2016).

As an aside, the Ernest Renan essay mentioned in the review that follows, titled "Intolerance in Scepticism," can be found in the 1896 book *The Poetry of the Celtic Races, and Other Essays*. The essay is a critical review of the "post-Hegelian" philosopher Ludwig Andreas von Feuerbach and his book *The Essence of Christianity*. Feuerbach was part of the clique of writers that included Max Stirner. Stirner also criticized Feuerbach for his "inconsistent atheism," in *The Ego and His Own*. It is curious that the review below asserts one essay about one left Hegelian's work can debunk the entirety of *Might is Right* and the sources it drew from. The great breadth of sources was not detailed until the publication of *Might is Right: The Authoritative Edition*, which cites hundreds of sources and references among over a thousand footnotes and other material.

A Bogus Book
The Tocsin

Vol. II. No. 78.   MELBOURNE, THURSDAY, MARCH 23, 1899.   ONE PENNY.

A BOGUS BOOK

"The Survival of The Fittest
or
The Philosophy of Power."

From Chicago. Addressed,
    "The Editors,
        "'Tocsin,'
    "Chief Justice Madden and others," has come along a book enti-
tled as above by Ragnar Redbeard, L.L.D. which Tolstoi is reported
to have stated, "has positively filled him with alarm and dread." *The
Tocsin* is sorry for Tolstoi.

The book is a wordy, windy exposition of Individualism. It is
described as "No ordinary book. Nothing like it has ever been permitted to see the light since A.D. 300." Which is tommyrot, as the
volume is but a garish hotchpotch of many books issued since that
date and before this precious work. For scientific criticism of them,
nothing is more concise and comprehensive than Renan's fine essay
on "Intolerance in Scepticism," published about fifty years ago.

The author, Gingerbeered Redrag, commences by proclaiming
"Death to the weakling, wealth to the strong." Wealth is his ideal, and
in his advocacy of its pursuit he challenges "the wisdom of the world,"
and "stands forth to interrogate the 'laws' of man and God." All of
which he does on the principle that the weakest shall go to the wall
and the fittest shall survive.

As an illustration of the logical justification of his theory, he cites Darwin and his whole theory of physical and animal evolution. He overlooks the fact, however, that if the fittest individuality survives, so does the fittest idea. The very fact of its survival is proof of its fitness. So his condemnation of Socialism falls flat, for Socialism survives and flourishes, so does Christianity, in its Socialistic sense. *Si monumentum requiris, circumspice.*

The book, which is evidently a claptrap production sent forth to capture shekels, is about as incoherent a wail as has ever been sent up from the Individualistic Camp. It reminds you of Marshall-Hall at his worst, and the more so since its author confesses to having been inspired by Nietzsche, Dahn, Gutzkow, and other German scribblers whose logic-chopping capacity obviously transcends their knowledge of human nature. Anyhow civilization has become too complicated to permit of its many problems being solved by primitive methods and a resort to merely brutal principles.

This Ragnar Redbeard is not convincing in any sense. "If," he says, "you would conquer wealth and honor, power and fame, you must be practical, grim, cool and merciless." What a gospel to preach to a world of fifteen hundred million! As if each individual doing his or her best on the most approved and advanced principles "Made in Germany" could hope to achieve "wealth, honor, &c., &c.!" It is a much simpler and more practicable thing for each to seek Justice. If it is to be a fight between Individualists for Wealth, &c., and Socialists for Justice, we shall see who will prove fittest and who will therefore survive.

Australian Socialist Drinking Club
Kevin I. Slaughter   **2023**

The Hegemony Club was one of many turn-of-the-century socialist groups in Australia. Teri Merlyn, in their "Writing Revolution", lists the following: Tocsin Clubs, The Victorian Socialist's League, the Victorian Labour Federation, the Labour Church, the Women's Political and Social Crusade, a Yarra Bank Propaganda Group, the Richmond Working Men's Clubs, the Knights of Labour and a Marxian Club.

The Bulletin for June 16 1900 announced:

> A new god for Victoria! The Melb. Hegemony Club, a fortuitous collection of unattached Stunners and Drangers of the guerrilla red-democrat persuasion, who conduct proceedings very successfully without the assistance of chairman, officers, objects, or rules...

In a July 19 1900, a column on the group that appeared in *The Tocsin*, had the following note:

> HEGEMONY CLUB.
> Last Thursday's meeting was mainly occupied with saddling Mac with the worry of arranging for the catering, etc., for our Bastille shivoo.
>
> On Saturday, the 14th, this duly took place at the Hibernian Hall to the delight of a large and enthusiastically rebellious company.
>
> The room was neatly ornamented with the device "1789-1900, Liberty, Equality Fraternity," argent upon *gules*. The meeting was international in character, there being present French, Germans,. Austrians, an Outlander champion of the Transvaal, and the "Consul for South America." Among, other songs we had the Marseillaise in English, then in French; a verse from "The Oarmaguole," in French; a tenderly sweet Slav sigh for home and country, in a language alien to the Russian (this was a sort of Slavonic "Esile of Erin"); a beautiful song in Italian; a song from Goethe, in German; a verse of a Taal satire on Cecil Rhodes in Taal itself; "The March of the Workers," by Morris; "The Leader of the Future," by Desmond; a Collingwood song, by Anon; several recitations of a hair-raising type; a few

stirring speeches, including a wonderful impromptu, rising to genius, to the sublime, in parts, from J. A. Andrews (author also of several rousing songs sung during the evening), and a lightning sketch of the Transvaal by our visitor from South Africa. Victor Daley's Tocsin song was also recited. We were so embarrassed with our riches that we had very regretfully to turn out the gas before "The Death of Joubert"and Robert Burns' "Tree of Liberty" were reached. The proceedings conducted themselves admirably, Hegemonywise; without chairman, toastmaster, waiter, or programme. It was a night to be remembered — one of those rare foregatherings of irreconcilables and rebels, talked of for years and years after, and sowing new and greater rebellions in the tyros fortunate enough to have been present. We hope that the fruits of the evening, as far as Australia is concerned, will show that the taking of the Paris Bastille in 1789 was worthily and appropriately celebrated by the Melbourne Hegemony Club in 1900.

Additionally, in a section for meeting notes provided by members, is this item:

> Arthur Desmond, New Zealander and Australian, author of "The Leader of the Future," and other stirring verses, was also the author of that remarkable much talked of American brochure, known as "Might is Right; or, the Survival of the Fittest," by Dr. Ragnar Redbeard.

All of this is significant for two reasons: 1. It was never a *secret* in Australia that Arthur Desmond wrote under the name Ragnar Redbeard, 2. Socialists still sang his revolutionary verses at their meetings after the publication of *Might is Right*. It was only in America that Desmond was truly successful at hiding his real name and keeping it separate from his many pseudonyms, and it is only in the past few decades that there has been any real attempt of radical socialists, communists and anarchists to separate themselves from Desmond's magnum opus *Might is Right*. Desmond and his writing have always been part of and celebrated by revolutionaries and radicals, with only infrequent dissents. For over 100 years his writing was promoted by the vanguard of radical left politics, and not just on the fringes, but central, significant figures, in every country he spent any time in.

Redbeard's Rough Stuff

C.F. Hunt   **1918**

From *The Truth Seeker*, December 28th, 1918.

To the Editor of The Truth Seeker:

The Crucible, Seattle, Wash., advertised a book, "Might Is Right," by Ragnar Redbeard, and seemed to approve of the fiendishness of Nietzsche and the frightful crimes which the Huns recently practiced as ordinary daily activities. Now The Crucible says the article (offering the book for sale) "was a clever bit of satire."

I would strike out the word "clever." The article was a clear recommendation of the book, and the advertisement still appears. Perhaps some kind of joke money is accepted for the book.

The love of horrors can be left with the followers of Moses, Samuel, Joshua and David. After exterminating whole peoples, the Lord told them: Thou hast done well. Unorthodox conquerors show clemency. Liberal papers must not disgrace themselves by beastly ethics, especially since murder, rape and robbery, as natural virtues, have been tried and found wanting ; have been crushed as menaces to civilization; and by their own principles are not Right lacking Might.

"Might Is Right" just as the preacher goes to the circus, to learn the evil of it. Redbeard is simply an ignorant cave-man who is sure the evolutionary process stopped with himself. Because beasts fight, the horrors of human fighting will always be beautiful; and kindness, benevolence, equality, which have somehow evolved, are vices of weakness. Read in the preface:

"The natural law is tooth and claw. All else is error, it rules all things; it decides all things. The victor gets the gold and land every time. He also gets the fairest maidens. And why should it be otherwise? Why should the delights of life go to failures?"

Thus maidens are mere "delights," not humans with rights. Page 98: "Women are frail beings . . . they must be held in subjection. Man has captured them. Woe unto the race if ever these lovable creatures become rulers or equals of men."

Ragnar's ignorance is proved by his love of big words, used at random. Page 79: "Allegorically speaking, the clothes we wear, the houses we live in, the food we eat, the books we read, have been carved (by force) out of men's bones and flesh. Literally, they are the hides, sinews, flesh, pulp, and outer wool covering of captive animals, transmuted by human slavery into garments, lumber, implements, thoughts, shoes, dinners. And behold it is good. ... This world is a gruesome butcher shop, where slain men hang in rows. Man is the fighting, roving, pillaging, lusting, cannibalistic animal. The King of the Great Carnivore."

Page 99: "Daughters . . . are given to men who have proved their inherent manhood in carnivorous (flesh-eating) combat."

He probably means "sanguinary" or "bloody"; but what can we expect of a cave-man? The social lesson is that fair daughters must be given into slavery to a superman who has killed and eaten at least one man.

Ignorance of medical facts appears on page 78: "The transfusion of blood of animals in human veins . . . is regularly practiced by medical men." The Encyclopedia Britannica says of transfusion (vol. 27, page 939): "Only the blood of man must be used."

Well, lumber is not made from animals; nor is humanity compelled to get its ideals from carnivorous animals. The mildest and most useful animals could not be induced to eat an organic creature, nor rend one unless in self-defense. If we must learn of animals, take for teacher the patient cow or playful horse. Combat has been found to exterminate, rather than preserve, the fittest.

C. F. HUNT

"We Understand the Redbeard Philosophy"

James Rowan   **1918**

The following 1918 letter was recorded as part of an indictment for *THE UNITED STATES OF AMERICA vs. GEO. O'CONNELL et al.* This is one of the many cases brought against the Industrial Workers of the World, also known as the I.W.W. or "Wobblies". It has been said numerous times that the egoist book *Might is Right* was a "Wobbly Bible" and here is a letter from a significant figure in their movement to another. The official I.W.W. website gives the following in a biographical sketch: "James Rowan began organizing in the Lumber Industry for the IWW as early as 1916, witnessed the Everett Massacre, and became involved in the great IWW LWIU organizing campaigns from 1917-23. During this time he became to be known as the 'Jesus of the Lumberjacks.'"

Cook. Co Jail
Chicago, Ill.
Jan. 10th 1918

John Grave,
    Fellow worker
    I see your name and address in the "Worker" so will drop you a line, to let you know how things are at this winter health resort. There are quite a bunch of us here and the conditions are fairly rotten, but in spite of all the drawbacks, the bunch all seem to be enjoying their vacation pretty well. It is sure interesting to meet the boys from all the different parts of the country, and hear how the movement is going ahead in the different sections. The boys from the west compare favorably with the rest, and it seems they have a better understanding of the movement. The spittoon philosopher element and the anarchists seem to be pretty numerous in the east.
    Well John we sure gave the lumber trust a wallopin last summer. That was the first time they were ever whipped and they were sure whipped to a finish, the lumber jacks are lining up to beat hell. Last month over thirteen hundred joined. It looks like we will soon

control the lumber induetry. They are still fighting us in desperation but we have got a strangle hold on them and their case is hopeless. Of course we expect nothing else than to be jailed after taking part in a strike like that for we know that a rebellious slave is the worst criminal in the eyes ot the masters but what the hell of it. When we understand the Redbeard philosophy, as you and I do, we only laugh at an old sissified can like this. It is pretty feeble institution to try to break up a strong job organization with. It shows how feeble are the minds of the rulers, and how little they grasp the significance of this movement. What do you think of the Bolsheviki? What they can do in Russia, we can do in this "land of the Free."

Well, John I hope to hear from you soon.

Will cut her short now as I am not sure whether you will get this or not. I know you fellows have trouble of your own down there. None of the Edmonton fellows have arrived here yet but we expect Jim Manning any time. The other Manning was turned loose today. Also expect Turner in near future.

With best wishes
Yours for the One Big Union
James Rowan.

James Rowan "Leavenworth Prisoner #13113"
Care of: https://weneverforget.org/tag/james-rowan/

Voima On Oikeus
Covington Hall

1917

This translation of Covington Hall's poem "Might is Right" is from *Proletaari Laulija* (Proletarian Singer), the 1917 Finnish translation of *I.W.W. Songs: To Fan the Flames of Discontent*. It was published by Workers Socialist Publishing Company of Duluth, Minnesota for American immigrant workers and members of the Industrial Workers of the World. The same company published the newspaper *Industrialsti*, which was founded in 1914 under the original title *Sosialisti*. Shut down in 1975, it was the last non-English IWW periodical. Of historical note is the conviction of Edward Ollikkila in Thunder Bay in Canada. On October 9th, 1919, he was arrested and pleaded guilty having "in his possession... certain prohibited publications, namely *Ajo* (The Forge), *Industrialisti*, and *Proletaari Laulija*." He was given hard labor for two years or a $2,000 fine.

VOIMA ON OIKEUS

(Might is Right.)
(Covington Hall'in mukaan.
Sävel: Sven Dufva.

On voima kautta aikojen
Halinnut maailmaa;
Tää sääntö ompi muinainen
Sen nytkin nähdä saa.
Kun voima onpi oikeus,
On silloin kansain kuninkuus;
Totuudenkin tunnustus,
Ja valtain mahtavuus.

Niin, voima oli oikeus,
Kun Kristus surmattiin;
Ja Craccus sekä Spartacus
Kuin sortui hurmeisiin.
— Se sääntö sama silloinkin

Ragnar Redbeard

Kun Ludlow poltettiin,
Kun Mesaban ja Buttenkin
"Työlakot murskattiin."

Ja voima oli oikeus
Kun Ranskan Communin,
Tuo vallan hirmu hallitus
Hurmeisiin hukutti.
— Näin silloin, samoin vieläkin,
Tään säännön saman nähdä saa;
Sen Ferrer, Hill ja Littlekin
"Verellään todistaa".

Niin voima ompi oikeus,
Kuin surman loukot saa;
Se riistovallan ahneus,
Orjille rakentaa.
Vuostuhansien sorranta,
Piina ja kidutus vaan
Voiman oikeudesta
"Vain onpi todistus".

Voima onpi oikeus
Myös silloinkin kun saa
Suuri vallankumous
Joukkomme pelastaa.
— Voima oli oikeus,
Kun Ryssan Nikolai,
Hirmu-itsevaltius,
Virastaan potkut sai.

Voima orjain verraton
On päällä koko maan;
Siis kaikki yhteen unioon
Voimaamme tuntemaan.
Voima onpi oikeus,
Voimaamme käyttäkää;
— Silloin orjain vapaus
Meill' perinnöksi jää!

No Detail Too Small!

Trevor Blake   **2023**

This small detail from *Sayings of Redbeard*, published circa 1927, appeared previously in 1910, published in *Crime and Criminals,* by the Prison Reform League.

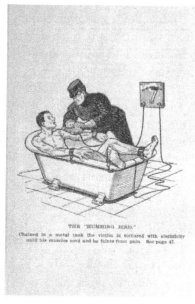

↑ From *Sayings of Redbeard*, The House of Gowrie, (n.d.).

↑ From *Crime and Criminals* by the Prison Reform League, Los Angeles: Prison Reform League Publishing Company (1910).

That is all!

DORA MARSDEN

Born in Marsden in 1882. In 1900 began teaching at Owens College, where she met Christabel Pankhurst and other suffragists. Dora joined and became a leader in the Women's Social and Political Union (WPSU) by 1908. The following year she resigned as a teacher and became a full time agitator for the WSPU, graduating from suffragist to suffragette. She was sentenced to two months in prison for vandalism in 1909: she refused to wear prison clothes and served her time in the nude, even wriggling out of a straightjacket that had been forced on her. After a hunger strike she was released and continued to agitate. She disrupted political meetings (including a speech by a young Winston Churchill). The WSPU "promoted" her to a clerical position to temper her agitation. Dora, meanwhile, had grown tired of the "skirt movement" and sought a liberty beyond feminism.

In 1911, Dora founded *The Freewoman* (1911–1912), a periodical described by one forgotten nobody as "a disgusting publication... indecent, immoral and filthy." Financial troubles led to a re-launch as *The New Freewoman* (1914). And an ever more keen search for liberty led to a re-launch as The Egoist (1914–1919).

In the 1920s–1930s Dora wrote three books: *The Definition of the Godhead* (1928), *The Mysteries of Christianity* (1930) and *The Philosophy of Time* (published only in 1955). During the writing of these books she went from a self-imposed isolation to confinement in a mental hospital, where she spent the remainder of her life.

Dora Marsden for the Prosecution . . . . **.97**
Manchester Evening News   1910

The Freewomen of New York . . . . **.99**
The Forum   1912

Dora Marsden, *unser aller Mutter* **101**
Trevor Blake   2022

Dora Marsden Ephemera **102**
(Various)

A Rare Portrait. **105**
Votes for Women   1910

A Rare Portrait. **106**
The Huddersfield Daily Examiner   1993

Dora Marsden for the Prosecution
Manchester Evening News   1910

Dora Marsden was known to appear in court on the defense for furthering through militant action the principles which she was known to support; suffragette. Here is a lesser-known example of her appearing in court on the attack. From the *Manchester Evening News* for 14 February 14, 1910. Dora and Mary Gawthorpe would both leave suffrage to establish *The Freewoman*. Mabel Capper (1888-1966) was one of the first suffragettes to be force-fed during imprisonment. She maintained a lifelong commitment to her principles, and a life-long connection to Mary Gawthorpe and her family.

SOUTHPORT ELECTION SEQUEL

POLICE COURT PROCEEDINGS

The Southport Police Court was crowded today when John Aspinall, Peter James Halsall and James Sumner were charged with assault by Miss Mary Gawthorpe, Miss Dora Marsden and Miss Mabel Capper, suffragists, and there was a further summons brought by Miss Dora Marsden and others against Councillor Dr Arthur W. Lemont for damage to a flag.

Mr. Greaves Lord, barrister, prosecuted and Mr. Overend Evans defended.

Sir George Pollard, MP, presided over a full bench of magistrates.

The summonses for assault were taken first. Mr. Greaves Lord said the assault was committed on Southport election day.

Miss Gawthorpe, Miss Marsden and Miss Capper along with other ladies attended the polling booths in Southport for the purpose of furthering the principles which they were known to support. Between four and five o'clock they arrived at St. Simon's and St Jude's Schools one of the polling booths. Limont took a flag from the car. It was through this that the whole bother commenced. Limont tore the flag off, waved it in the ladies' faces and threw it into the crowd. One of the ladies got out of the car at the polling station and was roughly treated by the crowd. Two others got out to assist her and some further bother ensued.

It was arranged that Miss Marsden should board a tram car and go down to see the Chief Constable for help while Miss Gawthorpe and Miss Capper remained at the school. Miss Marsden failed to board the tram car and was hustled back by the defendants. Miss Gawthorpe was pushed violently against the car and Miss Capper was next taken up by the defendants and lifted right over the head of Miss Gawthorpe and thrown into the car head first with her legs in the air.

A number of witnesses were called in support of Mr Greaves Lord's statement.

CASE FOR THE DEFENCE

Mr Overend Evans for the defence said that with regard to Dr. Limont it was monstrous to bring a gentleman of his position into court on such a paltry charge as damage to a flag. The proper place for the action was the County Court.

Joseph Robson, an ex-county constable and who acted on the day of the election as a special constable, said he asked the ladies to move on when they drove up in the motor car because they were obstructing. Everything was quiet until they came. He did not see any violence.

Mr Greaves Lord promptly reminded the witness that he had previously signed a statement to the Chief Constable that violence had been used and he then admitted that one of the ladies was pushed into the car head over heels.

William Johnston, election worker, said he carried one of the suffragists to the car and he did not consider it unnecessary violence. A lady named Higham an election worker said she herself early in the morning put one of the suffragists out of the yard because she was telling people "to keep the Baron out." The witness admitted that she wanted to "get the Baron in."

MAGISTRATES' DECISION

The charge of assault was dismissed and the other charge was withdrawn. Sir George Pollard announced that there were eight for dismissal and one against.

Councilor Austin, another magistrate, protested against this announcement and said that there ought simply to have been a declaration made by the chairman of case dismissed. As a matter of fact, to be quite correct, there were five for dismissal and four against.

Mr. Jones another magistrate also said there were four against dismissal.

The Freewomen of New York
The Forum

An enthusiastic review of *The Freewoman*, edited by Dora Marsden, from *The Boston Evening Transcript* of Boston, Massachusetts (January 1st, 1913), page 22. The uncredited author references "A New Prophetess of Feminism: Dora Marsden" by Frances Maule Bjorkman, from *The Forum* (October 1912). The final issue of *The Freewoman* was Volume 2, Number 47 (October 10, 1912). It was re-launched as *The New Freewoman* (1913) and finally as *The Egoist* (1914-1918). Also included here is an excerpt from an unpublished letter from Dora Marsden to Bjorkman, regarding what is likely the first expressly egoist / individualist public event held on North American soil.

Dora Marsden, a Feminist Disciple of Nietzsche
by Frances Maule Bjorkman
From *The Forum* (October 1912)

The feminist movement has evolved its 'superwoman' or, rather, the superwoman is the ultimate expression of that new philosophy of feminism preached by the very latest prophetess, Dora Marsden, in her daring "humanist review," the London *Freewoman*. With its mid-October issue, *The Freewoman* ceased temporarily to exist, but we shall probably witness its reappearance shortly in a still more arresting form as a "significant and compelling sign of new developments taking place within the woman movement." John Galsworthy and Francis Grierson contributed to its columns. H. G. Wells was not only a contributor, but a "constant reader." The editorials won the applause of Havelock Ellis and the respectful attention of Bérnard Shaw. The extraordinary young editor, Mrs. Bjorkman, remarks, "shot into the philosophic firmament as a star of the first magnitude. Although practically unknown except as a settlement worker and a suffragist before the advent of *The Freewoman* in November, 1911, she speaks always with the quietly authoritative air of the writer who has arrived." Her amazing staff reviewer Is a girl of eighteen.

   The Freewoman has voiced a philosophy as egoistic and undemocratic as Nietzsche's. It discards the ordinary. The difficult and dangerous creed by reason of which it exists will be rejected today, says Dora Marsden, by three women out of every four.

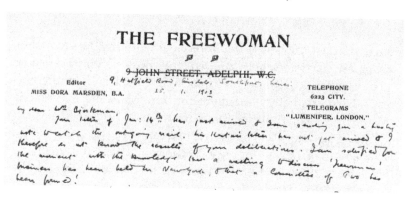

25. 1. 1913

My Dear Mrs. Bjorkman:

Your letter of Jan. 14th has just arrived & I am sending you a hasty note with the outgoing mail. [Miss Kenton's?] letter has not yet arrived & I therefore do not know the [?] of your deliberations. I am satisfied for the moment with the knowledge that a meeting to discuss "Freewoman" issues has been held in New York, that a Committee of Two has been formed!

Dora Marsden, *unser aller Mutter*

Trevor Blake   **2022**

> Lande der Freiheit aus. („Das Jerusalem, das droben ist, das ist die Freie, die ist unser aller Mutter". Gal. 4, 26.)
>
>
>
> ("The Jerusalem that is above is the freewoman ; she is the mother of us all." Gal. 4. 26.)
>
>
>
> To
>
> THE GREAT NAME
>
> HUSHED AMONG US FOR SO LONG
>
> of
>
> HER,
>
> HEAVEN,
>
> THE MIGHTY MOTHER
>
> of
>
> ALL.

Dora Marsden (1882 – 1960) broke with what she called the "skirt movement." She saw that the leaders of the Womens' Suffrage and Political Union may have called their journal *Votes for Women* but their actions were in the service of the leaders of the Womens' Suffrage and Political Union. Dora wanted a new movement that was openly self-interested, openly promoting only the freedoms and abilities of the individual. She had read Stirner, and knowingly declined to call her movement egoist. She called her movement the freewomen, and the title of her 1911 journal was *The Freewoman*. The following may be the inspiration for that name.

In *Der Einzige und sein Eigentum* (1845), Max Stirner quotes Galatians 4 verse 26 in saying: "*Das Jerusalem, das droben ist, das ist die Freie, die ist unser aller Mutter.*" Stephen T. Byington translates the passage in his 1907 translation of Stirner, *The Ego and His Own*, as "The Jerusalem that is above is the freewoman; she is the mother of us all."

Dora references the passage again in the dedication to her book *The Definition of the Godhead* (1928): To / THE GREAT NAME, / HUSHED AMONG US FOR SO LONG / of / HER, / HEAVEN, / THE MIGHTY MOTHER / of / ALL.

Dora Marsden Ephemera

(Various)

Three previously undocumented ephemeral mentions of Dora Marsden, editor of *The Egoist*.

First, two lines from the book-length poem *The Atheist* by George Bedborough (London: Garden City Press, 1919):

THE ATHEIST

BY

GEORGE BEDBOROUGH

Dora Marsden writes well and so do her friends,
But The Egoist sometimes to crankiness tends.

LONDON :
GARDEN CITY PRESS
37, GT. RUSSELL STREET, BLOOMSBURY, W.C.
AND AT LETCHWORTH
1919

Second is an advertisement for *The Egoist* which appeared in *Bruno's Weekly* Vol. III No. 19 (October 25, 1916):

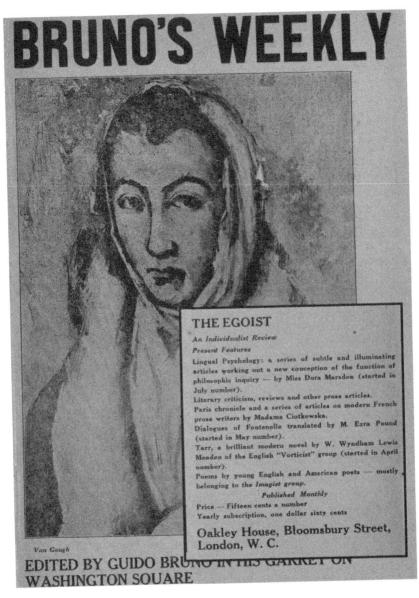

BRUNO'S WEEKLY

THE EGOIST

An Individualist Review

Present Features

Lingual Psychology: a series of subtle and illuminating articles working out a new conception of the function of philosophic inquiry — by Miss Dora Marsden (started in July number).

Literary criticism, reviews and other prose articles.

Paris chronicle and a series of articles on modern French prose writers by Madame Ciolkowska.

Dialogues of Fontenelle translated by M. Ezra Pound (started in May number).

Tarr, a brilliant modern novel by W. Wyndham Lewis Meaden of the English "Vorticist" group (started in April number).

Poems by young English and American poets — mostly belonging to the *Imagist* group.

Published Monthly

Price — Fifteen cents a number

Yearly subscription, one dollar sixty cents

Oakley House, Bloomsbury Street, London, W. C.

Van Gough

EDITED BY GUIDO BRUNO IN HIS GARRET ON WASHINGTON SQUARE

Finally *The Freewoman* advertised in *The Conservative and Unionist Women's Franchise Review* No. 10 (January–March 1912). "The Conservative and Unionist Women's Franchise Association is opposed to the demand of a vote for every woman; they only ask that sex should cease to be a disqualification, and that women who fulfil the same conditions as men should enjoy the same political rights and privileges":

A Rare Portrait
Votes for Women   1910

This image of Dora Marsden from *Votes for Women* has not been
reprinted since its first publication on July 22, 1910.

A Rare Portrait
The Huddersfield Daily Examiner 1993

Undated photograph of Dora Marsden from *The Huddersfield Daily Examiner* for February 8 1993.

Suffragette Dora Marsden: her courage "was accentuated by her fragile beauty and her diminutive stature"

BENJAMIN DeCASSERES

Benjamin DeCasseres (1873-1945) was a writer in many forms, from editorial to poetry, and the author of many books and booklets. Born in Philadelphia, PA, he dropped out of school and got a job as an office boy for the Editor-in-Chief of *Philadelphia Press* newspaper. At age 16, he was promoted to proofreader and occasionally wrote editorials and reviews.

In 1899, at age 26, he moved to New York and got a job with the *New York Sun* as a proofreader. His first freelance article was published in 1902 and shortly thereafter he began contributing to Elbert Hubbard's various magazines, often ghostwriting.

In 1906 he moved to Mexico to work for the English-language edition of *El Diario*, but that only lasted a year before he moved back to New York. He worked and lived there for the rest of his life. He passed away in 1945.

> "We have had in the last two thousand years Christian-baiters, Jew-baiters, free-speech baiters, free-thought baiters, and now in this country we are afflicted with the Pan-baiters. They chase the great god from the eating places, from literature, from the 'movies,' from the stage, from the painted canvas, from the great poem, from the hearts of the human... Pan-baiting is the veritable business of our lawmakers and sectarian pundits. If they ever discover that sunlight intoxicates they will attempt to gouge the eyes out of the God of Day himself." —Benjamin DeCasseres, "The Pan-Baiters," from *The Judge*, April 3rd, 1920.

Emmeline Pankhurst **109**
Benjamin DeCasseres   1914

Pyrrhonism and Acatalepsy **112**
Benjamin DeCasseres   1911

Balzac **114**
Benjamin DeCasseres   1911

The Borrowed Mirror **116**
Benjamin DeCasseres   1907

Emmeline Pankhurst
Benjamin DeCasseres

1914

From *The Fra*, Vol. 12 No. 6, (March 1914), pp. 182–183. *The Fra: A Journal of Affirmation* was published by Elbert Hubbard (1856–1915).

All new movements are deadly. They are elemental. They are born of some sublime moral, intellectual or physical transgression.

The renewers and renovators, the precursors of every renaissance, bring not peace, but a sword. War is as eternal as matter and motion and change. Christs, Luthers, Darwins, Hugos, Whitmans, Wagners, come to dynamite and destroy. They are in the intellectual sphere what earthquakes, lightning and thunder are in the physical world. Everything repeats the elemental laws of physics. Everything that is great and mighty and cleansing is attained with blood. Everything that is sublime is a form of wickedness raised to the highest power.

Great prophets, newcomers, heralds, hurl tiles from the house-tops and plant in secret places giant time-bombs that may not do their religiously murderous work for fifty years after they are planted; but they work automatically and irreparably. Christ planted a time-machine that blew to fragments the ancient world. So did Luther, Rousseau, Voltaire and William Lloyd Garrison.

The Stamp of the Absolute

There are no moral values; there are only esthetic altitudes. From the fourth dimension of the imagination, great criminals are the equal of great saints. So that they both be sublime, every Napoleon will top every Spinoza, and a Miltonic Lucifer will rank with a Mary Magdalen. Emmeline Pankhurst belongs to the Elect.

She bears the stamp of the absolute. That is, she has the winged prophetic soul, the destroying passion of great humanitarian geniuses, and she uses the flaming speech of an avatar. The old regime is gone and that barbaric Jehovah with it. The modern mind rises out of the ruins, a vision of flame and thunder, chanting the glory of life, the divinity of impact, sex for sex's sake, and the greatness of Woman.

Pankhurst is, whatever you say, the flower of that great reaction against other-worldiness begun by Ingersoll, Bradlaugh, Stendhal and Nietzsche. Matter and force forever and forever are divine. The eternal bloodsucker, the Spiritual, must be crucified again. Away with the vampire "saviors" of the race! To the rack and the crucifix with those who blaspheme against matter! Stamp out forever the libelers of the sun, the stars, the lily! Only the innate pornography of the cowled and ascetic spiritualists have made of woman's body a reek and a pig-sty. This is a practical world, and the Practical is an epic. Every denier of the flesh and matter is led into his velvet heaven to the fanfare of a thousand pig-grunts, like Saint Anthony. Matter is the only mystery and the only reality. The future always belongs to the materialist. The spiritualist is a reversion, an atavism, a perversion of the time-instinct and the sex-instinct. Pankhurst has talked of Here and Now.

The Return From Nirvana

The Feminist Movement, of which Emmeline Pankhurst is the soul, represents also a violent reaction against the intellectual. It is the return from Nirvana. From the ice-bound abstractions they come crashing into the jungles of the concrete. Come across with the ballot and our natural rights! They celebrate and immortalize every-day life.

On the anvils of their lyricism they forge the beauty of the coming time with the raw material of the ugly world that surrounds us.

They are revenants of sanity and health in a world of alcoholic poets, anemic doctrinaires and boudoir essayists like Cassiodorus. The Feminist manifestos, which are flung broadcast over the world in three or four languages, ring like a mountain call. A style veined with the red health of youth. It is, indeed, the Red Terror of Health which has flung itself into a tuberculous and shamble-footed world. An atavism? Yes. It is a reversion to Eternal Youth; a reversion from the Vampire-Ideal to a hot-blooded Reality. An atavism truly! From the peaceful catacombs of the state of Grace, the suffragists invite us to the hallucinating perspectives of perpetual transgression. They are very ancient are these Pankhursts as ancient as the first pantheists who kissed the earth passionately and "hurled their lances at the sun."

"Freakishness" is the word that Stupidity uses in the presence of the rare. Well, Pankhurst is freakish!

Where are there any standards for anything? Where are they to be found—in what brain, in what secret mountain of the moon, in what revelation? The rare and the normal are contradictions in terms. The beautiful and the popular are antithetical conceptions. Standards shift as the brain shifts. Values change with each new emotion. The thought or feeling that is not anarchic in its incipiency will never be great. Everything great and luminous and immortal is born a Cain. Has Emmeline Pankhurst broken the law? Yes! And there are more that need smashing.

Fear nothing. Scorn death. Live life ecstatically. Measure your grandeur by the number of things your Will has crushed. Open wide the nostrils of your consciousness and draw in the wild salt savor of your instincts. Sobriety of any kind is a curse. Battle and intoxication, pain and victory justify life. Rub acid in your wounds so as to madden and stiffen your Will. Keep the pistol of purpose pressed against the temple of your weakness. Be cruel to no one but yourself. Each day carry a dead self on the pike of your Will. The soul is a monstrous gadfly that stings matter and mind to incessant action and transformation.

Emmeline Pankhurst is immortal before her death.

Pyrrhonism and Acatalepsy
Benjamin DeCasseres

1911

From *The New York Sun* (January 3rd, 1911).

To the Editor of *The Sun*
Sir:

Mr. Gallatin's remarkable letter in this morning's Sun wherein the general bankruptcy of all scientific speculation is pointed out is a straw which shows us the drift of a world current. Are we going back, or going forward, to the doctrine of the Acataleptics? This doctrine was the doctrine of the incomprehensibility of things. Pyrrho is the supreme acataleptic among the ancients; Anatole France and Rémy de Gourmont are the supreme acataleptics among moderns. All opinion will finally become heretical. To say "I know" will be to put the stamp of ignorance on oneself. If catalepsy is a possession, acatalepsy is a state of ultimate freedom. The brain of the acataleptic was an eye that through an eternity of time focused its vision in an infinite number of directions. The world to it was a whimsey. Nothing can be proven; nothing can be disproven. "Eureka!" was uttered by a madman. And if this is true of science, why not of religion also?

Flux and reflux—what do we know? Belief of any kind is a species of hypnosis. Certainty is the superstition of sensation. Time is an illusion, said Kant. Eternity is a word, says Science. Each thing is only a mask for some other things—infinite veils. Names are the tags we put on incomprehensible objects. There is a Rabelaisian hilarity on the face of Nature, as if it would say, "Presto! Behold me! Behold me not! Whatever is is not. That is my supreme jest."

Pyrrho and Montaigne arrive at ecstasy; the ecstasy of indifference. They lived in a world without longitude or latitude. The "I think, therefore I am" of Descartes would have been written by Pyrrho "I think, therefore I think I am." At the touch of this Prospero of negations the dogmas, religious and scientific, that we have nuzzled to our bosoms turn to fantastic mockeries. If Shakespeare created a world, Pyrrho and Montaigne destroyed a sidereal system. "Only the absurd is true," whispers Satan into the ear of St. Anthony in Flaubert's great dream poem. The senses lie, the brain lies, the heart lies, consciousness lies. How do we know they lie? Because another lie proves it. Man, the eternal Sancho Panza on his ass of Certitude!

In the retorts of the brain of the Supreme Sceptic cosmologies and gods are melted. He puts his finger on Death and says: "Not proven." He puts his ear to the heart of Life, thundering in its Gargantuan hulk of matter, and says: "Thou art only a seeming." Crescent and Cross, Scarabee and Dragon are fused and evaporate in the mighty menstrum of this alchemic mind. One folly is pitted against another folly, one monstrous illusion rises to comfort another monstrous illusion. Mr. Gallatin's reasoning solves the universe. The iron gates of God are papier mâché. Plato's eternal Ideas are plaster paris. The celestial seraglios of Mohammedanism are sacrosanct pigsties, the "Mansion in the Skies" is in cinders. The First Cause of theology is a metaphysical spite wall. The Ego of the Romantics is a huge dummy swollen taut with flatulent German metaphysics. Anarchism, socialism, agnosticism, all isms, are merely mirage, the affabulations of temperaments. They are the passing incarnations of the Incomprehensible, the yawns of Maya, the god of illusions.

If, then, we are bankrupt in intellect, in faith, what attitude? While the battle rages the acataleptic polishes a spyglass. He belongs, then, to no army. He is not interested in victory or defeat. Only the spectacle enchants. His brain is ascetic; his eye alone is gluttonous. He is at Troy, at Waterloo, at Gettysburg. It is all the horseplay of ants on an unimportant star. And Aristotle, Plato, Nietzsche, Schopenhauer, Spinoza, Hobbes, Leibnitz, Pascal and Hegel? They are interesting but unimportant, like life itself.

According to Mr. Gallatin to know will be the cardinal heresy. Ah! This little man who comes all ahuff into the world and solves the riddle of Being! This self-constituted aide-de-camp to the Infinite! This sculpted piece of protoplasm who, with arms akimbo, budgets his prejudices into the ears of the Sphinx!

The smile on the face of this ironic nihilist—the Pyrrhonian sceptic—is a smile that is more terrible than the grief of a world. He is the grand dissociater of ideas, the surgeon of illusions, a snow that blankets all growing things. Anatole France, before his descent to socialism, and Rémy de Gourmont are the modern prophets of this creedless creed. With the bare bodkin of incredulity they have slain the eidolons of the ages.

"What do I know?" asks Montaigne. "Just that," answers enigmatically Pyrrho from his tomb.

Balzac
Benjamin DeCasseres

1911

From *The Backbone Monthly*, Vol.2 No.1 (January 1911). The editor, Thomas Dreier (1884 – 1976), was an American editor, writer, advertising executive, and business theorist. Drier wrote: "This wonderful appreciation of Balzac originally appeared as a communication to *The New York Sun*, in which had been raging a literary battle as to the respective merits of Anthony Trollope and the master Frenchman. It is reprinted here because of its inspirational tone—its strength—its power of constructive analysis."

To compare Trollope to Balzac is to compare the well-bred scenery of Prospect Park to the wild, almost blasphemous beauty of Yellowstone Park. Trollope is Philadelphia, Balzac is Paris. Trollope is a museum, Balzac is a Sphinx. Trollope is the Eden Musée, Balzac is Olympus. Trollope is an imaginative Pepys, Balzac is the Dante of intellect.

Like Shakespeare, Cervantes, Kant, Goethe, he was clumsy. He was too great for his medium of expression. He was a Titan piping on a reed. His mind apprehended the All in a glance, and he could only stammer when he would have fulminated. His brain was blockaded with ideas. A whirlwind of visions, emotions and prophetic dreams blew through his mind–and wrecked it. When he conceived a book he felt that a universe was bulging for birth in him. He was impatient. He could not, like De Maupassant and Flaubert, spend years building a bed for the perfect accouchement. He pitched his stuff out savagely, obliquely, helter skelter, for Debt and Death were at his heels. And that is what we call his "obscure style."

Minds of the first order never seek for style. They are so overwhelmed by the vigor and vanity of their own natures and visions, are so completely mastered by their ideas that they smash all rules. In this class are the authors of the sacred books of the East, the Book of Job and "Don Quixote." Rabelais, Shakespeare, Goethe, Nietzsche, Wagner, Rodin, Walt Whitman, Blake, Gorky and Balzac–were they "stylists"? Who cares?

Balzac was a seer. His eye pierced all the veils of matter. He was the biographer of the human soul; he tops Shakespeare and Molière. He wrote the history of the Second Empire, but it might have been the chronicle of any other period in the world's history. Under the tatters of Time he saw the eternal Man; he ripped from out of its network of circumstance and convention the quivering race instincts and held them naked and bloody above his head. He plunged his finger through the tissues of flesh and muscle, through the thin mask that civilized man wears, and touched firmly the impelling secret motive. Holding his finger firmly on the secret spot while his subject screamed in shame and humiliation, Balzac turned an ironic and triumphant grin on the spectators.

The "Comédie Humaine" is Balzac's answer to the Sphinx's question, "Unriddle me existence." And his answer was another riddle. At bottom Balzac was a Hindu of the eider age. The great sin of man is Ego, the self, the individualized, differentiated I. The soul of man, to Balzac, was an inferno of lusts, a city of sadic visions. Man is an inutile appanage of an aimless, protean Force. And man only rises to greatness when he looks at us through the mask of a Vautrin. For in this world, according to Balzac, the Will to grandeur and the Will to goodness are at everlasting war.

To Balzac the world had been invented so that he could analyze it; good and evil were only points of orientation, alternate coigns of vantage from which he, reporter for the gods, could watch the fray. Vautrin is Balzac, from one point of view. Good and evil existed because the gods needed sport. Or, as Heine said, because the Aristophanes of the heavens was in need of mirth.

Balzac's mind was a huge piece of the universal Mind, in which we exist merely as infusoria. His brain was not a mind, it was a breeding place. He accouched his characters, whereas Trollope only created his. The germ of every variety of human being existed in the mind of Balzac. Like Goethe and Shakespeare, he was an encloser of all species, ideas and methods. He gave birth to such vital beings because he was giving birth to particles of himself. That is the supreme mystery of genius.

Balzac's imagination was eucharistic. He lived the life of the race vicariously. A vision as profound as Sophocles, the godlike apprehension of Aeschylus and Shakespeare, a power of co-ordination as great as Beethoven and Herbert Spencer, the titanic vigor of a Goethe and a Walt Whitman, and the superb unarithmetical mockery of an Aristophanes and an Ibsen—he, too, was a Cosmos.

The Borrowed Mirror
Benjamin DeCasseres

From *Cosmopolitan Magazine* Vol. XLII No. 5 (March 1907), p. 479.

"What will other people think?" is the most cowardly phrase in use in society.

Only weak men stand in fear of the censure of the neighborhood.

Whatever is great in life brings down censure upon the head of the doer.

A man who lives, moves, and has his being in other people's opinions has not risen to the level of animal intelligence. The dog and horse are at least sincere and natural in all their acts.

Why not dress your life before your own mirror?

Look for your reflection in your own mind. There is a secret judge of all your acts within you. Conscience is your private opinion of yourself.

Why borrow a thing when you possess it yourself? What does it matter what others think of your actions? What do you think of them?

Some men crouch, crawl, and skulk all their lives. They are cowed by a whisper; their purpose is shaken by a look. They run like sheep before somebody's opinion, though they would return blow for blow if they were attacked on the highway.

They are larded, greased, and curled wax figures. Whenever they move you know that Public Opinion has pulled a wire somewhere. When they speak you know what they will say. They are not men enough to offend.

The ogre, Public Opinion, slays more originality and individuality than all the barbarous superstitious codes put together. It is the modern Moloch before which we all meekly bend.

That shameful hypocrisy which permeates society everywhere is born of the fear of other people's opinions. Sincerity and plain speaking are at a premium everywhere. We lie from morning until night, and pretend to things we abhor.

Turn once upon that lazy braggart, Public Opinion, and see it scamper away.

It is our latest idol, the modern social Juggernaut.

6
FRIEDRICH NIETZSCHE

Friedrich Nietzsche (1844–1900) is exceptionally well documented elsewhere, and *Der Geist* has very little to add. For the few who somehow see his name here first, here is that very little. Nietzsche was a philosopher and an author born in Prussia. In *Thus Spoke Zarathustra* (1883), Nietzsche wrote of the overman, one whose right comes from his might. In *Beyond Good and Evil* (1886), he wrote of the individual and not external moralities as the basis for ethics. In *The Antichrist* (1888), he wrote of the destruction of religion by men willing to say God is dead.

Nietzsche was never asked if he had read Stirner, and he never wrote that he had read Stirner. It seems possible Nietzsche read Stirner. After more than a century of debate on the possibility that Nietzsche read Stirner, *Der Geist* offers the final judgement: *it doesn't matter*. Let us read and consider both in their similarities and their differences. Egoists and Overmen who ignore their ego and their will in favor of a mere pedigree are confused from the start. Most of our "Union of Egoists" (Seklew, Redbeard, Tucker, *et. al.*) freely sang of either or both according to their own purposes.

Nietzsche and a Braille Stirner for Hellen Keller **119**
Benjamin R. Tucker   1914, 1927

"Will Nietzsche Come Into Vogue..." **121**
Thomas Common   1910

The Works of Friedrich Nietzsche **129**
Holbrook Jackson   1912

Alexander Tille Reads *Egoism* **133**
Harold Hiller   1914

Nietzsche and a Braille Stirner for Hellen Keller

Benjamin R. Tucker   1914, 1927

In the first letter, Tucker discusses the responsibility of Nietzsche for the first world war. In the second letter, sent over a decade later, the proposition that a braille edition of Max Stirner's book could be made for Helen Keller. The Union of Egoists has determined that a braille edition of Stirner was not produced at that time. Benjamin R. Tucker (1854 – 1939) was the publisher of the journal *Liberty* as well as the first English translation of *The Ego and His Own* by Max Stirner. George Schumm (1856-1941) was an individualist anarchist writer and translator. In 1884 he launched the *Radical Review* and worked for Benjamin R. Tucker for three years publishing *Liberty*. He translated John Henry Mackay's *The Anarchists* in 1891 and assisted Steven T. Byington in translating *The Ego and His Own*. William Archer (1856–1924) was a Scottish writer and theatre critic, based, for most of his career, in London. He was an early advocate of the plays of Henrik Ibsen, and was an early friend and supporter of Bernard Shaw.

October 2, 1914

Dear Mr Schumm:

I have heard from the Hetzels (as indeed you have written me yourself) that you think me mistaken regarding Nietzsche's responsibility for the war. I enclose a letter from Wm. Archer to Gerhardt Hauptmann, showing that not only archer, but Hauptmann himself, takes my view.

How do you account for the writings of Treitschke, Bernhardi, H. S. Chamberlain, and others? Are not these evidently an outgrowth of the reading of Nietzsche? And have these not dictated the military policy of Germany? It is no answer to argue that Nietzsche meant this, or that, or the other. The apologists for E.G. use the same argument when confronted with the acts of her disciples. In both cases there may be some slight misunderstanding of the teacher, but I think that both may fairly be held responsible. Certainly, if Hauptmann is misled, the Kaiser may well be. And I think that Archer's quotation from Nietzsche illustrates with sufficient exactness the German treatment of Belgium.

October 11, 1914

(Excerpt)

I enclose some clippings. That signed W. Bulloch expresses my view of the actual results of Nietzsche's influence, while not failing to do justice to Nietzsche by showing that these results have not taken the exact form that he looked for or would have approved.

In reading these clippings, of course, you will entertain no suspicion that I share the tendency of the writers to champion Christian influences. I am the same egoist as always. The egoism of Germany does not disturb me; given the Germans' domineering instincts, I am glad that they have no scruples about satisfying them; and my answer to their brutality would be to slay them as speedily as possible and put them forever out of the way, in order that egoists of another type, who love peace and liberty, may enjoy their preferences undisturbed.

November 25, 1927

Dear Mr. Schumm:

I wrote you of the proposition of the National Institute for the Blind regarding 'The Ego and His Own'. It turns out to be a bit less encouraging than the first letters to Fifield indicated. Not bad, though, after all. What it amounts to is this; a copy is to be cut in raised type, by hand, by a volunteer, for Helen Keller, and a duplicate is to be put in the general library of raised type for the blind. I suppose, then, that Helen Keller is interested, or, if not, that some enthusiastic person hopes to interest her.

One sees now in Russia the perfect realization of "peace at any price," a land that knows not hate, the flowering of the gospel of universal love, Tolstoyism gone to seed. What a spectacle does that unhappy country present today! Simple, stupid, sodden; reeking, rotting, rampant; a deliquescent nest of life that crawls and creeps, she melts, she sprawls, she slops, she stinks! A gigantic Camembert, in the last disgusting stage.

Friedrich Nietzsche

"Will Nietzsche Come Into Vogue..."
Thomas Common
1910

From *Current Opinion* (July 1910). Thomas Common was one of the early translators of Nietzsche into English, and was part of a small group of advocates of Nietzsche in the Anglosphere. Common appeared in the egoist journal *The Eagle and the Serpent* (1889–1927). Common also published his own journal, *Notes for Good Europeans*. Egoist titan Benjamin R. Tucker described *Notes for Good Europeans* in Volume XIV Number 23 of his journal *Liberty* (September 1904): "The contents of the magazine are both good and bad—depending on the 'point of view.' The subjects range from a sober discussion of Shakespeare and quotations from Bernard Shaw and others to an unmeasured laudation of the rantings of Ragnar Redbeard." This article shows Nietzsche's foothold into the American psyche was still unsure, though he'd had a number of prominent advocates in the US. H.L. Mencken was certainly Nietzche's most high-profile early American advocate, and in Mencken's circle of friends were two others: James Huneker and Benjamin DeCasseres. It was Huneker who probably introduced the greatest number of Americans at that time to the other iconoclastic German, Max Stirner, in his New York Times article that announced the new publication of *The Ego and His Own*.

Will Nietzsche Come Into Vogue In America?

The Works of Friedrich Niezsche. Edited by Oscar Levy.
   The Macmillan Company.
* *Nietzsche in Outline and Aphorism*. By A. Orage. Chicago:
   The A. C. McClurg Company.
* *The Gist of Nietzsche*. Arranged by H. L. Mencken.
   Boston: John W. Luce & Company.
* *Men Versus the Man*. A correspondence between Robert
   Rives La Monte, Socialist, and H. L. Mencken, Individualist. Henry Holt & Company.

The neurotic but strangely fascinating "philosopher with the hammer," Friedrich Nietzsche, has begun to invade this country. "Nietzsche is in the air," Dr. Joseph Jacobs remarks in the *New York Times Saturday*

Review. Six volumes of a projected complete translation of his works are now in currency here. A handbook on Nietzsche, written by an Englishman, has been re-published in Chicago. A collection of epigrams, entitled *The Gist of Nietzsche*, is offered by Henry L. Mencken, of Baltimore, author of *The Philosophy of Friedrich Nietzsche* and champion of that same philosophy in a newly issued written debate with a Socialist. Mr. Mencken, who undoubtedly has done more than any other writer in this country to spread Nietzsche's gospel, calls attention to the fact that "Nietzsche has been breaking into print of late with conspicuous assiduity":

> The theological reviews denounce him in every issue as a natural son of Judas Iscariot and Lucretia Borgia. The yellow journals connect him with 'waves of crime' and 'the decay of the churches'—spelling his name Nietsche, Neitzche, Nitshe, Neatzsche, Nitysche, Nittsche, Neitzshy, Nitschie, Nietzschy and Niscksy, according to their degrees of ignorance. In the uplift magazines he is becoming as prominent as Dr. Woods Hutchinson and Judge Ben B. Lindsay. In the *New York Nation*—last stronghold of the Harvardocentric theory of the universe—his name is mentioned in the same paragraph with those of immortal Rollos and Waldos. Only *The Ladies' Home Journal* and *The War Cry* have yet to find him out.

The slow but persistent growth of Nietzsche's fame is one of the intellectual romances of our time. When he died, bereft of reason, ten years ago, no one could have predicted the extent of the influence he was to exert. Nothing less than a library of comment, interpretation and criticism has grown up around his name. Some of his phrases have become household words. His books, which were printed at his own expense and hardly taken seriously during his lifetime, have since been pronounced masterpieces and translated into many tongues. A German critic, Robert Mayer, speaks of Nietzsche's rhapsodic poem, *Thus Spake Zarathustra*, as the greatest production of German literature since Goethe's *Faust*. Bernard Shaw goes even further in calling the same poem "the first modern book that can be set above the Psalms of David at every point on their own ground."

Two American estimates of Nietzsche of more than usual penetration appear in recent issues of *The Independent* and *The Smart Set*. The first, by Edwin E. Slosson, excels as a piece of criticism, while the

Friedrich Nietzsche

second, by Mr. Mencken, is strong on the positive and affirmative side. While differing widely in their estimates of Nietzsche, these writers both agree in conceding his compelling power.

Dr. Slosson takes as his point of departure a saying of Nietzsche's to the effect that "every great philosophy is the confession of its orig-inator and a species of involuntary and unconscious autobiography." If this aphorism of Nietzsche's be applied to himself, Dr. Slosson de-clares, the result is curious, for "never was there a greater contrast between the life and the creed of any man, moralist or immoralist, than existed in his case." The argument continues:

> The eulogist of the strenuous life, he spent his in teaching classical philosophy and in philosophizing. War he regard-ed as the mother of virtues and pity the greatest of crimes, yet his part in the Franco-Prussian war was that of hospital nurse. His ideal was the great blond beast, ruthless, self-as-serting, lustful, healthy, independent and dominant. He himself was frail, near-sighted, dyspeptic, neurasthenic, enslaved to drugs, celibate, timorous and retiring. He con-demned and denounced women as inferior beings, to be kept as slaves and toys, yet it was to a woman, his sister, Frau Forster-Nietzsche, that he owed not only his life, during the last eleven years, when he was as helpless and witless as a babe, but also the establishment of his reputation after his death, through the collection, publication and elucidation of his manuscripts.

If, then, Nietzsche's philosophy was in any sense his autobiogra-phy, it was the autobiography, Dr. Slosson suggests, not of his actual but of his dream life. "All he could never be, all men ignored in him, that he was worth to himself." The qualities he lacked appeared to him the greatest of all virtues, and the things he couldn't do seemed to him of all things the ones most worth doing. "We all," Dr. Slosson thinks, "have moods like this, a form of the natural attraction of op-posites, of our awe of the incomprehensible and our admiration for the unattainable." Moreover:

> Nietzsche was Hegelian in temperament. Every idea suggest-ed to him its opposite and he was equally attracted by it. He reminds one of the pith ball of the laboratory, that is first drawn to an electrified body and clings to it for an instant,

then is seized with repulsion and evermore flies from it. So Nietzsche is enamored in turn of Schopenhauer and of Wagner until he becomes charged with their spirit, and then conceives for them an intense aversion and antagonism. He treats even his own ideas in the same way, flying the next moment to the opposite pole of thought, becoming the iconoclast of his own idols. He was like most of us in seeing only one side of a thing. He was unlike most of us in seeing the other side of it soon after with equal intensity and exclusiveness. He never sees both at the same time in their real proportions and relationship. Had he kept to one point of view he would have exerted more influence over the world, but the fascination of his style lies in his vibrant thought. An Audrey Beardsley sketch, with its impossible masses of black and white, is more striking and sometimes brings out an idea better than a half tone.

As Dr. Slosson sees him, Nietzsche was the incarnation of the spirit that denies. The very fact that a thing was established or accepted was enough to incite him to attack it. Finding woman honored, he depreciated her. Finding the spirit of democracy everywhere, he denounced it as a delusion and a snare. In a civilization saturated with the Christian feeling, he preached the gospel of the AntiChrist. While the trend of social development ran overwhelmingly in the direction of a subordination of the individual to organizations that increase his efficiency, he advocated an individualism bordering on Anarchism. He objected even to the communism of opinion: "My opinion is my opinion; another person has not easily a right to it. One must renounce the bad taste of wishing to agree with many people." Altogether he was, in Dr. Slosson's judgment, about as negative and iconoclastic a figure as could be conceived.

But Mr. Mencken, presenting Nietzsche sympathetically, sees him from a very different angle. The great value of Nietzsche, Mr. Mencken would have us believe, lay just in the fact that he reacted from Christian doctrine and emphasized the values that Christianity blurs or ignores. He went back to paganism to recover the values that Christianity had lost. To quote verbatim:

Nietzsche's whole philosophy grew out of his early inquiries, as a student of Greek, into the spirit of Hellenism. It needed no long investigation to show that this spirit of

Hellenism was almost diametrically opposed to the spirit of Christianity. The Greeks, indeed, esteemed as virtues nearly all of the things banned by Christianity as vices and sins. Their notion of an admirable man was one who exhibited strength, ingenuity and what might be called assertive autonomy. A man who, on being smitten by a foe, turned the other cheek, would have excited their contempt. A man who, in the face of danger, threw down his arms and began to pray to the gods, would have made them laugh. They believed that life was a pleasant thing, and that it was worth while to fight for it. They believed in efficiency and egotism; they liked to do things—to rear great temples, to dance, to give gigantic shows, to make war, to amass wealth, to conquer.

To Nietzsche the Greek spirit was beautiful, the Judaistic spirit repulsive. The first was an assertion of the will-to-live, the second an attempt to escape from facing real life by preaching self-sacrifice, humility, altruism, and similar sentiments. These principles, he contended, were the logical outcome of the oppression and suffering endured by the Jewish race; they may have served an admirable purpose in their time and place, but when they were taken over by the nations of western Europe, they became a positive hindrance to all that is best in humanity. Mr. Mencken tells us:

> Nietzsche believed that if the dominant races of the present day could be rid of the outworn and unworkable moral code of the Jews, they would make far more rapid progress than the world has ever seen. Out of this idea grew his celebrated conceptions—the higher man and the superman. The higher man is merely an efficient and ruthless man who has rid himself of all pious cant and hypocrisy. He is not a predatory bully, as many critics of Nietzsche seem to think, but an intelligent progressivist, with an eye not so much to his own immediate advantage as to the ultimate profit of the race. He wars upon the unfit chiefly because he doesn't want them to contaminate the racial strain. He sees nothing honorable nor noble in poverty and humility, but only a confession of unfitness to survive. Let the weak die, he says, that the strong may not have them to drag along. Let the highest honors of the world go to those men who make the most successful war upon the forces and conditions which work against the

race—disease, climate, distance, time, terrestrial catastrophes, religions, superstitions, handicapping customs and laws. Not only to the warrior the honor, nor only to the emperor and millionaire, but also to the explorer, the pathologist, the revolutionary, the iconoclast, the immoralist.

Such, in crude outline, are the principal ideas of Nietzsche's philosophy as Mr. Mencken presents it. Is it, he asks, insane, as many would have us believe? He answers:

I am constrained to think not. In places it may tax the imagination, but in other places it makes an irresistible appeal to every reflective man. Twenty years ago Nietzsche was merely an interesting freak, but to-day you will find his notions elaborated in the writings of men whose sanity and title to leadership are unquestioned. Mr. Roosevelt borrowed copiously from Nietzsche for his essay on 'The Strenuous Life' —the most astonishing and most sincere of all his compositions. From Nietzsche Dr. Metchnikoff got his idea of a welcome death, and from Nietzsche Dr. Eliot got two-thirds of the propositions in his New Religion. Take away his Nietzschean flavor, and Shaw would be a mere harlequin. Rid the world of Nietzsche, and the year of grace 1909 could show no living philosophy.

The question arises, How far is the Nietzschean point of view likely to appeal to America? and the answers already given are manifold. Robert Rives La Monte, the Socialist opponent of Mr. Mencken in the debate already mentioned, finds in Walt Whitman all the healthiest elements in Nietzsche. His attitude suggests that Thus Spake Zarathustra will never supplant Leaves of Grass. Elbert Hubbard, on the other hand, looks to Emerson as a substitute for Nietzsche, and establishes (in *The Philistine*) this rather ingenious antithesis between Emerson and Nietzsche:

"Behold! I teach you the Overman," might have been enunciated by Emerson. The Overman of Nietzsche aimed at a beyond-man. The Overman of Emerson is to be evolved in man. Nietzsche sought to manufacture a God; Emerson sought to fabricate a man. Nietzsche conceived power as something that primarily flowed out of man; Emerson conceived it as

Friedrich Nietzsche

something flowing into man from the Oversoul—the shoreless sunken seas of the potential.

A Socialist writer in Wilshire's Magazine argues that if the "ruling classes" know their own business and want to stem the rising tide of Socialism, they will vigorously encourage the spread of Nietzsche's ideas. He is led to this view after reading Mr. Mencken's contribution to the Socialist-Individualist debate. It is not that he is won over by Mr. Mencken's statements, but they form, he thinks, the most logical argument against Socialism he has ever seen in print. He says further:

> However, they possess one fatal drawback in the fact that the bourgeois dare not publicly use them against Socialism. Even if their truth were admitted, their general and public announcement by the ruling class would be the signal for the almost instant destruction of the present order of things. The Nietzschean philosophy and the logical deductions therefrom cannot be proclaimed from the capitalist housetops. They constitute a true individualist philosophy which must remain the secret possession of the individual—a philosophy which is not for 'Men,' but for 'the Man.' The philosophical legacy left by Friedrich Nietzsche to the ruling classes of the world is a sword which, if they dare to draw publicly in their own defence, will turn upon and slay them.
>
> Mr. Mencken has but pushed to their logical conclusion views which in embryo are held by many bourgeois opponents of Socialism, but which, lacking his courage, they dare not develop, and are consequently forced to occupy a shifty, evasive and apologetic position, which rightly draws upon them the contempt and ridicule of the Socialist.

Dr. Joseph Jacobs, editor of *The American Hebrew*, seems to feel that Nietzsche's philosophy has a great future in America. Nietzsche, he points out, is aristocratic to the core, America democratic to the depths. Nietzsche is essentially Hellenic, esthetic, America is Hebraic, ascetic. Nietzsche's ideal is the solitude of the thinker, America's the solidarity of the people. "In the midst of the dissatisfaction with Americanism, which is characteristic of the age," Dr. Jacobs remarks, "it is refreshing, and, in many ways, instructive to consider a set of ideals so opposed and subversive of the American ones. Nietzsche is essentially one sided, but the side he presents happens to be the one hitherto unrepresented by American thinkers, and it therefore will have, in all probability, the greater attractiveness and influence on this continent." Dr. Jacobs writes further (in *The Times Saturday Review*):

> Against slave morality he opposes a master morality based upon the higher selfishness of the masterful men with the will to power. Napoleon, it may be remembered, made a similar distinction between 'la grande morale' and 'la petite morale,' and men of the type of Napoleon, Caesar, and Borgia, were the types that Nietzsche desired to see rule and destroy much of the rotting conventions of the hour. It is a mistake to think that they were his type of Supermen. They were only the anti-Christs to prepare the way.
>
> There is a rude, rough vigor in all this which is immensely attractive amid all the overturning of the ideals—Nietzsche calls them idols—of today. His virile thought ranges over the whole field of modern culture, except the economic division, on which he does not judge. His works are as stimulating as a storm by the seaside; the salt spray lashes but invigorates you. The supreme self-confidence with which he gives utterance to his paradoxes and cynicisms has specially an attraction for little minds, who flatter themselves they are little Nietzsches.

The *New York Evening Post* is unwilling to give Nietzsche much importance. It finds in the Anglo-Saxon mind a sanity which "feels instinctively that this boasted philosophy of strength is in reality a product of febrile weakness." In similar spirit Dr. Slosson affirms:

> It is not likely that he will ever be much read in the United States. Nor is there any reason why he should be. Nietzsche in Germany represents the reaction from Schopenhauer. Never having had the disease in this country we do not need the antidote. It is inevitable that we, like the rest of the world, should be influenced more or less by some phases of Nietzschean thought, but it will not be directly.

Friedrich Nietzsche

The Works of Friedrich Nietzsche
Holbrook Jackson

1912

From *The Bookman* Vol. 41, March 1912. Holbrook Jackson was a writer and socialist. He was part of the early Nietzscheans in England that included Oscar Levy, Anthony Ludovici, A.R. Orage, and others. Holbrook's book *The Eighteen Nineties: A Review of Art and Ideas at the Close of the Nineteenth Century* (1913) is useful for an appreciation of his time.

The Complete Nietzsche.

One cannot contemplate the completion of the English translation of the works of Friedrich Nietzsche without feelings of gratitude towards the practical enthusiasm of Dr. Oscar Levy who has guided so remarkable an enterprise to success. At the outset, the production of a complete set of Nietzsche's works in English was not without commercial hazard, but the results must indeed be gratifying to all concerned for (and it will come as a surprise to many people) no less than seven of the eighteen volumes comprising the edition are in a second, and three are in a third edition. That would indicate the existence of a public seriously interested in Friedrich Nietzsche, for it may be surmised with some certainty that the light interest aroused by journalistic exploitation of the challenge of his thought, and the tragedy of his life, has long since been surfeited, and those who skim over the surface of philosophic fashions are engaged elsewhere. There are, as a matter of fact, a great many people who feel, rightly or wrongly, that Nietzsche has a message for them; and their number is still respectable after it has been written down by the subtraction of those (and they are still many) who misuse or misunderstand him, drawn as they have been to his work by his apparent, but apparent only to the dull-witted, advocacy of moral license, and his childish and often irritating insistence on a desire to write only for the elect. To say you write for the elect is the surest way of attracting the mediocre. But, whatever, the status of Nietzsche's public there is little doubt that his thought and ideas are at length receiving something like acceptance in this country, or rather, we are at length in the heyday of surprise at the daring of the great German psychologist, although long after he has ceased to startle our continental neighbors. But up to the present, his direct influence has been small, what real influence he has had on English writers has been indirect, coming through French, German, and Italian authors who have written under his spell. It may be indeed that Nietzsche will not affect us as he has affected others, for we have become inured to the flaming aphorism of revolt in this country by the genius of Mr. Bernard Shaw, a thinker bearing many superficial resemblances to Nietzsche, though fundamentally opposed to him. So similar at times have these two thinkers been that shallow critics have hinted rather broadly as to Mr. Shaw's continental inspirers. The author of *"Man and Superman"* is strong enough to be his own first line of defense, but it is interesting to note, in the light of past criticisms of his originality, that the publication of Nietzsche's autobiography, *"Ecce Homo,"* actually lays the German open to the charge of having plagiarised the Irishman! In this autobiography, which is, by the way, one of the most remarkable and inspiring books ever written, Nietzsche repeatedly uses the egotistical gags which have been the stock properties of Bernard Shaw's drum and trumpeting for something like a quarter of a century. Before G.B.S. an autobiography like *"Ecce Homo,"* with such chapter headings as "Why I am so wise," "Why I am so clever," and "Why I write such excellent books," might have evoked an admonitory leader in The *Times*, and scare headlines in the Daily Mail; but familiarity with that method of self-expression has, as usual, produced indifference.

This is not the place or the time to interpret the Nietzschean idea, even if one could grant that place or time were ever proper to such an endeavor, which is doubtful. No interpretation of Nietzsche can have anything but a purely subjective value. Nietzsche has ever been his own best interpreter, but he becomes doubly so by the publication of *Ecce Homo*, which, with a stroke of the pen as it were, robs all his friendly commentators of their validity. All that need be said in a general way about Nietzsche, either in elucidation, in extenuation, or even in praise, is said in this wonderful book, and it is said on the authority of the only final authority, Friedrich Nietzsche himself, that is why Dr. Oscar Levy might have stayed the energy of his translators at the translation, and added himself the few necessary bibliographical and biographical details which are really all the preface each volume requires; not that the existing prefaces are incapable, they are unnecessary. Beyond a natural feeling against being talked to by what might be called conscientious Nietzscheans, before beginning one of the Master's books, I have none but feelings of gratitude for this splendid monument to the genius of the deepest and the

Friedrich Nietzsche

highest thinker of our time. The volumes themselves are convenient and quietly dignified both as to type and binding.

The completion of the English translation of his works gives us in this country the first chance of drawing for ourselves a full-length portrait of Friedrich Nietzsche, and we are helped very considerably in this task by "*Ecce Homo*," which is at least a three-quarter portrait of the artist by himself. In this book he not only reveals his own ideas one by one in a sort of organic relationship with each other, but he reveals himself also in relation to them, and here they do not always square well together; particularly in the philosopher's aspiration to be a satyr rather than a saint, for Nietzsche was by constitution the latter. He admits to never having had a desire, and from what we know of his life we can believe him: perhaps even Nietzsche was sentimentalizing when he patronized the satyr. His love of health also is unrelated to his condition, or rather related contrariwise, for, of course, it is not the first time an invalid has written vehemently of health. Such inconsistencies are forced upon readers of Nietzsche, not because they affect his philosophy, but because in so intensely personal a thinker they affect your view of him. The fact that his sanity gave way just after he had written "*Ecce Homo*," in 1889, has been used by many writers as an argument against his ideas, but the relationship, in this case, is very remote. Nietzsche was undoubtedly sane when he wrote his books, he wrote nothing after his mind gave way. It is conceivable that even the strongest of minds might break beneath such pressure as Nietzsche could bring to bear upon himself, for he was no formal thinker; he did not codify and co-ordinate the already thought-out, he constantly, made tracks into the unknown, and it is inconceivable that his ideas should be finally condemned and repudiated because of that. It may be unusual to say instinct is superior to reason; it may be illogical to stigmatize morality as decadent; it may have been wrong of him to prefer Dionysus to Christ or satyr to saint; his objection to ideals may have been inconvenient; his deep sense of the formative value of tragedy may have been unpleasant, and his dream of superman, absurd. But neither the charges of being unusual, illogical, wrong, inconvenient, unpleasant, or even absurd, are sufficient, severally or collectively, to convict a man of insanity—or there are very few of us sane. One idea, and one only, in the whole of Nietzsche's works touches the borderland, that is his conception of "eternal recurrence," but that idea, upon which one might brood oneself into Bedlam, is by no means peculiar to him, it exists in all its appalling emptiness in several writers and in many forms. Friedrich

Nietzsche is really much saner than most men, or perhaps than any man–he is as sane as the animals. It is his extreme naturalism, in an age conventional and artificial in idea and habit, that arouses doubts as to his sanity. Nietzsche is the naturalist of psychology–a sufficiently new thing to attract and repel. Like life, he is paradoxical, a yea-saying and a destruction. To accept life as a battle and take the consequences without revenge or resentment–and what does not destroy you creates you–that is the essence of Nietzsche. And after breathing the rare air of his thoughts one feels that the unwritten love is no longer unwritten, the contentiousness of life no longer a contention. He calls one of his books, "a book for all and none,"— Nietzsche may be described as a philosopher for all and none.

Friedrich Nietzsche

Alexander Tille Reads *Egoism*
Harold Hiller
1914

From *T.P.'s Weekly* Volume 24, Number 626 (November 17, 1914), p. 514. References a column by Holbrook Jackson and touches on Nietzsche and his appearance in the Anglosphere.

Nietzsche & Great Britain

Sir,—Is not the honour of being the first to bring Friedrich Nietzsche before British and American readers held by Dr. Alexander Tille, who when lecturer in the German language and literature at Glasgow University gave a lecture on the subject "Friedrich Nietzsche, the Herald of Modern Germany," on December 10th, 1894, to the Glasgow Goethe Society? Dr. Tille published at Leipzig in 1895 "Von Darwin bis Nietzsche, Ein Buch Entwicklungsethik."

He was the editor of Messrs. H. Henry's (J. T. Grein) edition, the translator of volume, "Thus Spake Zarathustra." If my memory was right, Dr. Alex. Tille's resignation was called for, on account of some pro-Boer expressions in a book, written in German and published in Germany.

I have before me a curious publication. (The Zarathustra number of "Egoism," Vol. III., No. 19, Oakland, California, November 28th, 1896. (Price five cents fortnightly, 50 cents a year.) The only number I have kept is devoted to the anonymous editor's remarks and disagreements and extracts from Dr. Alex. Tille's translation of "Thus Spake Zarathustra" (New York: The Macmillan Company)—e.g., "I protest against any consecration of myself and mine to the more finished man, except as incident to my pleasure.—Therefore I shriek 'fanatical devotion to Beyond-man' at Nietzsche. Nietzsche's introspective power is to such Indian skulled perception-chasers as myself a spell bound wonder—a grotto of home-driven discoveries, surprises and delights. Egoism's' purpose is to gain general recognition for a standard of Ethics and a Social Polity based on a logical extension of biological order into the social realm. Ethically, the Egoist knows nothing except the direct or ultimate satisfaction of the Ego. Politically the consistent Egoist can sanction no government of man by man save in the sense of defence. He is in short an anarchist—a Philosophic Anarchist."

I wonder whether "Egoism" is still published or went under before the Earthquake and Fire?

Messrs. Fisher Unwin, by taking over Tille's edition, publishing works on Nietzsche by Mencken, Mügge, etc., have rendered service second only to the publishers of Dr. Oscar Levy's edition. Prof. Andrew Seth (now Pringle-Pattison) had an article on Friedrich Nietzsche, his life and works in "Blackwood's Magazine," October, 1897.

— Yours, etc.,
HAROLD HILLER.
38, Jakeman Road, Birmingham.

ENZO MARTUCCI

Enzo Martucci (1904–1975) embodied the spirit of illegalist anarchism, drawing inspiration from Max Stirner. His given name Vicenzo Martucci he also wrote articles under the pseudonym Enzo di Villafiore. He maintained close affiliations with Bruno Filippi and Renzo Novatore. Hailing from Naples, Italy, he dedicated his life from adolescence until his passing to expressing and embodying his ideas.

After an initial marriage, he lived for twenty years with Renata Latini—the daughter of the anarchist printer Lato, who published *Umanità Nova*—with whom he had four children.

Throughout his journey, he faced persistent persecution from both the state and lesser radicals. Regrettably, only a scant portion of his prolific work has been translated for wider understanding.

In 2023 the Union of Egoists translated and published *The Red Sect*, as part of the Stand Alone journal project. It was originally published as *La Setta Rosa* in 1953.

A Sketch of Martucci **137**
Stephen Marletta
1967

An Excerpt from *The Red Sect* **141**
Enzo Martucci
1953

Martucci on Stirner **147**
Enzo Martucci
1967

Enzo Martucci

A Sketch of Martucci

Stephen Marletta

1967

The following biographical sketch was first printed in Sidney E. Parker's journal *Minus One* No.17, Jan-Feb.1967.

> "Anarchy is not a religion, a morality, or a social system, but a need of life. It teaches life to the free and is only realized by breaking all theological, ethical, and juridical restraints- including those so-called anarchists would impose."

> "I live for today and leave others to analyse tomorrow."

As Enzo Martucci received only a brief mention in *Minus One*, No. 15, I trust the following fragmentary account of his life and work will be of interest to readers.

Martucci was referred to as one of the few remaining torchbearers of individualist anarchist ideas. He is that-and more besides. Many have progressed and come to accept individualism via Tucker, Mackay and Armand to Stirner. Martucci got off to a better start it would seem. At an early age, through reading Plato's "Dialogues", he was impressed and influenced by the Greek sophists (Protagoras, Archilochus, Callicles) and later by Nietzsche, de Sade, Byron and Renzo Novatore (poet, individualist anarchist, his closest friend, killed by Carabinieri in 1922—see *Minus One*, No. 11). As the Greek sophists and Nietzsche had a great affinity with the philosophy of Stirner, you will understand what I mean.

At the age of 16, Martucci plunged into anarchist activities, much to the displeasure of his bourgeois parents, and was soon crossing swords with Malatesta in the columns of *Umanite Nova* in 1920. "Malateste", he says "was a good man, a sincerer revolutionist, but not an anarchist. He believed in the natural goodness of man and that with a change in social and economic conditions man would cooperate for the benefit of all." Martucci wrote at the time: "Man (in nature) is neither '*l'homo homini lupus*' nor '*l'homo homini angus*' but a mixture of both. The so-called good and the so-called bad...are not only determined by social causes, but also by biological and psychological causes. Malatesta believes in a future harmonious society. I have never done so."

Martucci accepted Stirner's teaching with its "rejection of all political and moral ties and its attacks on all general concepts such as 'right, virtue, duty, etc.' The individual himself in the only reality (sic). These concepts being mere 'ghosts', he rises above them by mastering himself. All relations entered into by him are freely chosen and exist only for his ego." Holding such ideas the clash was inevitable.

Like many rebels Martucci was born into a bourgeois family. His father's mother was the daughter of a count, who was the friend and architect to Ferdinand, the second of the Bourbons and king of the two Sicilies. Martucci was abandoned by his family at the age of 17 because of their strong objection to his ever-increasing anarchist activities. These subsequently brought him a terrible history of imprisonment which I will mention briefly.

He was imprisoned in a cell "four paces by four with a high window that permitted me only a glimpse of the sky. This I endured for six months." Taken ill, he was transferred to the prison infirmary after a plea from his mother who feared for his health.

When he was freed he returned to Caserta where he was wounded in a fight with fascists. Summoned to appear at the Court of Assissi he escaped to France and remained there until 1923 when the Italian government proclaimed a political amnesty. He went home, but for him, as he was soon to discover, there was no release. The Fascist government sentenced him to eight-year penal confinement (five of these he spent on the island of Lampedusa), five years of jail and three years suspended release.

He returned to Naples in 1942 and started a clandestine group of anti-fascists called "The Cavaliers of Liberty". An assault was planned on the offices of the Federation of Fascist Parties, but because of betrayal it did not materialize. Martucci found himself in prison once more. He was liberated in 1943.

As was the case with Malateste and Merlinc, Martucci also polemicized with his lifelong friend and collaborator, E. Armand "Whom I have always esteemed for his serenity and intelligence." The issues were many-particularly the one pertaining to "contract", Armand maintaining that one should not break a promise. This view is easy to understand to anyone familiar with Armand's early Christian-puritan-Tolstoyan influences which he seems never to have completely rid himself. As Martucci puts it: "Armand firmly claimed that the individual could not break his pact and leave an association without the consent of his associates, in which case he would be their slave, their property, the very opposite to what Stirner said."

I am with Martucci here. Our interests may be identical, but they may also differ.

The possessor of an active and formidable pen, Martucci's output has been extensive. His major works are: *Piu Oltre* a philosophical essay, 1947; *La Bandiera Dell'Anticristo*. (The Banner of the AntiChrist) a philosophical essay, 1950; and *La Setta Rossa* a criticism of Marxism, 1953. He wrote for Armand's reviews *l'en dehors* and *L'Unique*. When *L'Unique* ceased publication he contributed occasionally to a review called *Provisioni* published in Catania.

In May 1965 he began to publish his own paper and up to September 1966 had published thirteen issues in all, a total of over 12,000 copies which he distributed gratuitously throughout Italy and the world. This is no mean feat, and, considering present day printing costs and his not being a rich man, has meant considerable hardship. Each issue has a title of its own, in thick one and a half inch letters, pertaining to the main subject matter. How colourful and challenging some titles are! E.G. *Turbine* (Hurricane), *L'Anto di Satana* (Satan's Cavern), *Lo Scorpione*, *No Al Gregge* (No To The Herd), *La Sferza* (The Scourge) and *Prometeo*. Out of a device to evade the Italian printing laws a novel and magnificent idea is born!

Martucci has written; "The Germans have a saying 'many enemies, much honour'. If the judgement is true, then I am rich in honours. Because for forty six years everyone has been against me: fascists, Holy Church, socialists, anarchist communists. Persecuted and imprisoned under fascism, the persecution continues under democracy, only more insidious and hypocritical in form" (*La Sferza*, page one) Sometimes called "*la bestia nera*" (the black beast) it is easy to understand such unpopularity. If we know how dirty a word "Stirner" has become, Stirner and Martucci together must cause quite a stir.

Martucci is certainly fearless and has been so for forty six years. He relates how "one day I met and was surrounded by a gang of fascist toughs. They tried to force me to say "Down with anarchy and long live Mussolini!" Instead I cried "Long live anarchy and down with Mussolini!" I was taken to hospital with a broken head. In telling this incident to a lawyer acquaintance of mine, he told me how he was approached one day by a fascist thug who threw whit at him. He did not strike back. Instead he walked quickly home to clean himself. The lawyer, to save his skin, knew how to adapt himself to the world of today. But I don't know how to adapt myself. As for my skin, I don't give a damn." ("La Pelle", page four of *Lo Scorpione*).

A few years ago Martucci's companion for twenty two years, Renate Latini ("so sensitive and intelligent") died, leaving a great gap in his life. The details moved me, and the events leading up to her death I found very disturbing (The lack of care on the part of a hospital staff -Ed.)

I am more conscious now than I was at the beginning of my inadequacies in dealing with the life and work of Martucci. Not all will be in agreement with everything he writes. But none can deny his courage, fearlessness, intelligence, wide knowledge, learning and, if one may use the term, his cultural personality.

His writings, never obscure, are brilliantly clear and interesting and, when the occasion arises and demands, he is not afraid to voice his anger in a torrent of words. He is a master at marshalling his arguments. His aim is true and his thrust is clean cut.

In *Prometeo* (September 1966) he says that without some economic support he doubts if there will be many more issues of his "*numeri unici*."

Prometheus, the rebel who defied Zeus, suits Martucci well. For he has rebelled against the conditions that would dwarf him and hinder the growth of his individuality. I cannot think of Martucci's pen retiring while there is life in him, and hope that Hercules will come in the shape of economic support in order that he may continue, in his own words: "I publish my paper for the personal satisfaction it gives me. And because I like to express my ideas and lash at the sheep and the shepherds."

Enzo Martucci

An Excerpt from *The Red Sect*
Enzo Martucci   1953

"Born at Caserta (Naples) on March 20, 1904, Martucci became an anarchist at the age of 16 and ran away from his bourgeois home and studies. In his wanderings around Italy he met Renzo Novatore (Ricieri Abele Ferrari , an anarchist individualist, poet and illegalist who was killed in 1922 in a battle with the police) and from then on devoted himself to the advocacy of anarchist individualism. He was imprisoned by the fascist regime and its democratic successors: He wrote several books, including *Put Qltre* (1947), *La Bandiers dell' Anticristo* (1950) *La Setta Rosse* (1953, new edition 1969). From 1965 until the year before his death he issued his own paper, virtually written by himself. Each issue had a different title in order to evade the Italian printing laws. Several translations of his articles were published in *MINUS ONE* (among them the notable 'In Defence of Stirner') and a biographical article on him by Stephen Marietta appeared in No.17, Jan-Feb.1967.

Martucci had a strong and impetuous temperament and was a difficult person to get on with. All too often his writings digressed into attacks on people he believed to have wronged him and, like many individuals who have suffered real persecution, he tended to have a paranoiac attitude towards life."

—S.E.Parker

The following is a chapter is excerpted from Martiucci's book *The Red Sect*, translated into English for the first time by the Union of Egoists and published as part of the *Stand Alone* journal project.

Marxists on Trial

Stefano Kolnar was telling the truth. Communism wants to kill the soul. Bolshevik education suffocates all feelings in man and replaces them with blind fanaticism. Love, friendship, pity, passions do not exist in the communist; he has cut them off, destroyed his human essence, made a void within himself and filled it with the monstrous idea that dominates, alone and unchallenged. A slave to this idea, he wants to impose it on others and wants them to accept it as he has, without discussing, without evaluating, without subjecting it to the critical examination of intelligence. Dogmatic and sectarian, he attacks those who do not allow themselves to be converted. Whoever rejects the Marxist gospel and touches it with doubt is a heretic who must be fought with the same means the Church used in the Middle Ages to suffocate heresy. Whoever does not enter the red barracks or does not want to undergo their degrading discipline is an *enemy of the proletariat* or a *traitor*. Against these, the communist uses all weapons: when he can, he takes up his pistol as a GPU agent and shoots them in the back of the head;[5] and when he cannot resort to violence, he uses slander, lies, and cowardice erected as a system.

He has learned from Machiavelli and the Jesuits that the end justifies the means and does not shy away from the most disgusting and repugnant acts in order to achieve his goal. Fanaticized by the cause to which he dedicates himself completely, he is ruthless towards others and does not hesitate to sacrifice them in the interest of the *ideal*. If he has to push his wife into prostitution or ruin a friend or send a fellow fighter to jail to serve the party, he does it immediately without a moment's hesitation. Stalin denounced his political friends to the Tsarist police and had them arrested, thinking that their hatred against the state would increase in prison.

A Tuscan communist whom I met during exile, in order to corrupt a public security agent and obtain the clandestine transmission of letters from him and his superiors, offered him his young and attractive wife.

The Bolshevik has no heart, no soul, no feelings, he is below the brute which instinctively shies away from certain acts, while he does not shy away from anything and transcends any abjection that the advantage of the sect requires.

Bent by strict discipline, he renounces his personal freedom in the hands of his superiors and obediently follows all their orders. There is no infamy he would not commit, no humiliation he would not endure if his leaders commanded him to. A zealous follower, he obeys without discussion, he obeys solicitously even if they tell him he must be sodomized or that he must accompany his daughter to the brothel.

The interest of the ideal requires this passive submission and he bends his back and serves with pleasure, waiting to take revenge when Bolshevism triumphs and each of its followers can indulge their own lust for dominance, tyrannizing non-communists. Therefore, his

---

5   The Soviet State Political Directorate, *aka* GPU, was the Soviet intelligence service and secret police.

Enzo Martucci

fanaticism is not at all disinterested because he does not devote himself to an idea solely for the purpose of achieving justice or equality; rather, he dedicates himself to Bolshevism and lives only for it, hoping that the proletarian dictatorship will allow him to enjoy nationalized wealth and exercise authority, great or small, in society, depending on his rank in the party hierarchy. Whether a people's commissar or a Red Guard, a torturer in prisons or an executioner at Lubianka, the communist wants to be someone and crush someone under his own heel. Meanwhile, the heels of the leaders crush his chest and he endures it, disciplined and satisfied, because only in this way can the *idea* triumph and he can put a braided cap on his head.

The high and mighty leaders of the world revolution, together with their arrogant generals, hone their skills for the impending despotism by treating the faithful soldiers as mere slaves and subjecting them to various menial tasks. One of these poppies, a political exile confined to the island of Ponza, would recline in a beach chair and enjoy being fanned for hours on end by two young communist exiles, the B... sisters. He acted as a sultan in his harem, amidst the odalisques... And yet, no one delivered a swift kick in the ass to that deserter of the land.

Another leader who systematically appropriated the shares that the underlings paid for the Red Aid demanded that his comrades send their wives and sisters home to him.

The comrades obeyed, honored by the general's condescension, who after giving a sex education lesson to the women, taught history to the men and taught that Zarathustra was a Carthaginian leader who came to Italy with Hannibal and was killed by the Romans at the Battle of Zama.

Occasionally, among the fatherly communist figures, one meets an educated person like the hunchbacked Gramsci, the Torquemada of Italian Bolshevism; but generally, the red leaders are poor in spirit in whom ignorance is surpassed only by presumption. Professor Torelli (of what?) confused the thought of Kant with that of Gentile; and when I demonstrated to him that Kantian critical idealism is quite different from Gentile's absolute idealism, because for the former, there is the *noumenon*, the thing in itself, which we know only phenomenally, while for the latter there is only the human spirit that posits things, and he—the professor of bestiality—answered, with a smile of the superman, that I did not understand philosophy.

The Turin-born Roveda argued to a twenty-eight-year-old that there is historical evidence of the practice of sexual promiscuity in primitive societies. I replied that this evidence is lacking and that he was taking simple inductions from some writers who believed that certain customs of modern barbarians, such as offering a wife to a guest among the Eskimos, and certain historical customs, such as the sacred prostitutes of the Babylonians, the *jus primae noctis*, and the sacred defloration in Cambodia, were survivals of an ancient promiscuity. Roveda, not knowing what to say, turned his back and walked away indignantly. In reality, he did not know what the asserters of erotic communism of primitive times had written, who used arguments much more serious than his foolish sentences. He had never read Bachofen, McLennan, Lubbock, Morgan, Giraud-Teulon, and was ignorant of what Westermarck, Darwin, and Wundt had contrarily argued. Roveda had only read *The Origin of the Family, Private Property and the State*, the book in which Engels, copying Morgan, asserts, for the purposes of historical materialism, that in primeval humanity there existed the common possession of women, and that only when man formed a property did he want a woman solely for himself and imposed fidelity on her in order to transmit the goods to his own offspring. However, Roveda was ignorant of what other writers had opposed to his idol Engels; thus, with haughty confidence, he declared that there is historical evidence of promiscuity.

The same masters of Marxism, the luminaries of Bolshevik science, have also made absurd statements more than once.

Giovanni Gentile in his book *The Philosophy of Marx* observes that Engels has confused the Hegelian idea immanent in things with the Platonic idea of its transcendent nature. Engels in fact wrote in *Anti-Dühring*:

> "Hegel was an idealist, that is, for him the ideas in his head were not already the more or less abstract images of real things and events, but on the contrary for him things and their development were only the actualized images of the idea which already exists, before the world, somewhere."

This passage shows how well Engels understood Hegelian philosophy.

Karl Marx, who taught his disciples the art of calumny, wrote a book against Stirner entitled with an ironic motto: *The Saint Max*.[6] In

---

6   *The German Ideology* is a posthumous collection of writings by Marx and Engels, published in 1932. An excerpt of the third section was published in Italy in 1903 under the name *Il Santo Max*.

this book, the communist pope presents the author of *The Ego and His Own* as a metaphysician without knowledge, a weak imitator of Hegel, a philosopher of the German petty bourgeoisie, a "sentimental braggart" in theory, and a reactionary in practice.

In reality, Stirner's intelligence was superior to Marx's, and his spirit much more revolutionary. Stirner is, in history, the true anarchist philosopher, the only one who deserves this name.

Proudhon, Bakunin, Kropotkin, Reclus, are nothing but semi-anarchists, representatives of a compromise between individualism and collectivism, between socialism and anarchism. Theirs is only the anarchy of Paolo Gille,[7] the anarchy with discipline, the limited freedom of the individual who is no longer subject to the state but must subordinate himself to society for the satisfaction of his complete needs, and must always agree with everyone. In essence, they deny the state but deify society, as noted by Palante;[8] and they propose, against those who violate the future harmony, the harshest sanctions ranging from public contempt and general alienation, as advised by Kropotkin in *The Conquest of Bread*, to incarceration in the mental institution advocated by Malatesta in his pamphlet *Anarchy*.

Stirner, instead, is more logical as an anarchist. He believes that the individual is the only reality above which there is nothing else. Therefore, he wants the individual to fully realize themselves and satisfy their egoism, freeing themselves from the ideas that they have formed about the sanctity and inviolability of what limits them. God, morality, humanity, society, nation, and state are only ghosts that oppress the ego because it has created them, respects them, and serves them. But when the ego destroys them, when it makes them return to nothingness, then, having been freed from every spiritual and material tie, it will be able to live as it pleases, freely cooperating with its peers or fighting against them, depending on the needs, feelings, and interests that prevail in it at different times. It will be the *bellum omnium contra omnes*, tempered by individual alliances; but it will also be the natural freedom in which the individual can try to assert themselves by any means.

These are Stirner's ideas that can be accepted or fought against, but not falsified. One can believe with Basch that the individualist philosopher was anti-social and a disorganizer of the ties that unite human beings, or one can see in him the theorist of voluntary and

---

7   Paolo Gille, *Abbozzo di una filosofia della dignità umana* (Outline of a Philosophy of Human Dignity).

8   Georges Palante, *La sensibilità individualista* (The Individualist Sensibility).

spontaneous association that does not absorb the individual, does not pretend to eternalize itself, and does not deny the contrasts and struggles among the *unique*, strong, and independent. But one cannot claim that Stirner is a bourgeois philosopher when his philosophy constitutes the most radical subversion of the historical conception of life.

Stirner, the forerunner of Nietzsche, exalted egoism, pushed man beyond good and evil, and claimed the right to satisfy all personal passions, good and bad.

On the other hand, the communists want to suppress good passions and enhance bad ones: fanaticism, intolerance, cruelty, thirst for power. Their amorality, therefore, is to Stirner's amorality what the hypocritical perfidy of the snake is to the straightforward aggressiveness of the lion.

Stirner was an opponent of communism. "By the abolition of all personal property," he wrote, "(Communism) only presses me back still more into dependence on another, viz., on the generality or collectivity; and, loudly as it always attacks the 'State,' what it intends is itself again a State, a status, a condition hindering my free movement, a sovereign power over me. Communism rightly revolts against the pressure that I experience from individual proprietors; but still more horrible is the might that it puts in the hands of the collectivity."[9]

Marx opposed Stirner to better assert his doctrine and, as was his habit, resorted to slander, lies, and ridicule. However, what he wrote in *The Saint Max* is no more valuable than Torelli's confusion between Kant and Gentile and Engels' identification of the Hegelian idea with the Platonic one. And if the master, who had wit and culture, so often falsified the thought of others in bad faith, the disciples, who combine bad faith with ignorance, must necessarily arrive at the conclusion reached in his speeches by a Bolshevik whitewasher, confidant of the police and pimp of his sisters:

"In communism is our salvation. Everything that is not communist must be rejected, opposed, denigrated."

---

9   Max Stirner, translated by Steven T. Byington, *The Ego and His Own*, New York: Benjamin R. Tucker 1907.

Martucci on Stirner

Enzo Martucci

1967

The following essay was first printed in Sidney E. Parker's journal *Minus One* No.17, Jan-Feb.1967. It was translated by Stephen Marletta. Marless would receive letters from Martucci to Parker, and translated them into English so Parker could read them. The "Zoccoli" referenced repeatedly by Martucci in this article is the Italian scholar Ettore Zoccoli, who wrote a well-known general account of anarchism titled L'Anarchia, published in Turin in 1907. Ettore Zoccoli also translated the first Italian edition of The Ego and His Own, published as *L'Unico* in Turin in 1902.

In Defense of Stirner

Professor Ernesto Serafini, an academic who has polemicized with me before, now wants to start again and has written, amongst other things:

> You who boast of not being of the school of a Malatesta, but rather of Stirner, and who present the latter as a philosopher whose thought has a logic free from the contradictions one finds in the great Nietzsche, do not understand, nor wish to understand, the contradictions that also exist in Stirner. But Ettore Zoccoli answers you well in his book *Anarchy*. Indeed, he writes on page 410:
>
>> Although supposed to be politically and socially disintegrated, other individuals still remain. Well, says Stirner, it is up to the individual to make sure that those who surround him should be only a means to his ends. Briefly, it is an egoistic antimony raised by a metaphysician, that makes of each individual, at the same time, by a transcendental hypothesis, the supreme end and the most ignored means. In fact, while offering to the individual every possibility against his fellows, it denies them any possibility of being anything but mere means. Then it offers to

each of them in relation to the first individual every chance to reduce him to simply being a means. So that, at the same time in which an individual acts with the aim of considering others as means, he is faced with the action —not associated and therefore not multiplied, it is true, but numerically additional—of all those others who invert the role regarding him. The absolute autonomy of the individual is obliterated by the absolute autonomy of all others. This imperative of absolute egoism is either impossible if the atomistic aggregation of individuals represents even a system of force in equilibrium, or, if applied, would result in the reduction to nothing of any social aggregate no matter how elementary. It is an ethical imperative that even a cannibal would be ashamed to accept.

To Sarafini and Zoccoli it seems a contradiction to consider the individual as the only reality there is, having no other end than himself, and, at the same time, to accept that this same reality can be considered by others as a means to their ends. But, in substance, there is no contradiction. There would be if we referred to the same individual, if I should regard myself as the only existing reality who, as the supreme end, cannot be a means, and, at the same time, accept the demand of other individuals to serve them as means to their ends. Then I must choose if I am the ultimate end or the least of means. But since I regard myself as the end and the others as means, the two opposed values are not attributed to the same subject but to different ones, and so there is no contradiction. Can I not regard myself in one way and others to the contrary?

No, says Serafini, because others are individuals like you. But even if they are individuals like me, I cannot consider them as I do myself.

I know myself to be the only reality because I can sense myself. If I did not exist I could not sense. Therefore, I am. And I recognize not only my reality, but also an external "reality" — the material world, the spirit of other men, etc. But is this other "reality" imagined by me, or does it exist in itself? According to philosophic idealism matter does not exist, but is no more than a representation of the human spirit.

The universe is created in the mind which projects it outside

Enzo Martucci

thereby giving it objectivity, but retaining the power to differentiate and control it.

> There is no argument [writes Liebnitz] with which one can demonstrate in any absolute manner that bodies exist and nothing prevents our minds presenting them as well-ordered dreams, which we judge as real and for harmony we accept as equivalent to the truth.

But if the material world is a representation of the spirit in which it alone exists, the spirit of other men can equally, as can their bodies, be a representation of my Spirit in which they alone exist, together with the material world. Where is the proof that they continue to exist if I do not think or feel about them? And where is the proof that the universe continues to exist when I neither think of it, nor sense it, given that the only means of knowledge are thought and senses?

In this way, one arrives at solipsism and, in accepting it, I become certain only of my own reality, my own being, and I make myself my end and use as my means the world and other individuals, these being my creation which I can make use of as I will.

If, instead, as philosophic realism claims, the material world and human beings have an objective existence, not as I will, but in themselves, then these individuals look like me but are not the same as me. Each of us is a microcosm with his own way of feeling and thinking that gives him particular needs and aspirations which cannot always be satisfied without conflicting with others. In this case, because I live for myself and not for others, to respect and serve them in the way that I respect and serve myself is not obligatory for me. Since, they are different, therefore, I can very well use them as means to my own ends, even if I feel myself being used as means to an end.

Ergo: from the standpoint of all philosophical conceptions of reality, the contradictions which Zoccoli points out in Stirner's thought do not exist.

Nor does one find the

> egoistic antimony raised by a metaphysician, that while offering to the individual every possibility against his fellows, denies them any possibility of being anything but mere means.

Stirner says that, for the individual to realize his proper egoism, he can do all that he wants as long as he has the power. But he does not deny to other individuals the possibility of not being used as means. To these he says that they too can defend themselves and not let themselves be reduced to slavery by an aggressor who intends to make them his tools. He urges the attacked to counter~attack anyone who would make them into means. In time, as individuals developed their power to the maximum, they would control each other reciprocally—only the weak, the cowardly, the lazy (in other words, the ballast) —would disappear. Then there would remain a select humanity, which would form itself into an oscillating equilibrium, which would allow each individual, at least once, to realize himself integrally, to live as he felt and willed. In a social and civic world, however, based on a general mutilation, as Brunetiere called it; in a perfect world of which the utopians dream, in which each man disciplines himself to the maximum and always restrains and suffocates his own instincts and needs so as not to tread on his neighbor's toes—in such a world there cannot be an equilibrium, which implies a differentiation and opposition of elements and forces, but a stupid, softening harmony which would take everyone through life without ever having lived and would send them to the grave having seen nothing.

In the meanwhile, in the present world, imperfect but social and civic, a minority of tyrants and cheats impose themselves, making use of every kind of astuteness, violence, riches and power, and reducing everyone else to obedience and misery, trying to convince the oppressed with the nonsense of religion, metaphysics, ethics and legalism, to resign themselves and not to use any means of liberation. And fiercely condemning the few who rebel. So there is formed a stable disequilibrium with the result that a few are always on top, happy and ruling, and the rest are always at the bottom, suffering and serving.

If that which Zoccoli called "the imperative of absolute egoism" were applied, it would probably reduce all organized society to nothing, and would be willingly accepted by men restored to natural spontaneity and sincerity — men who find insufferable that social and civic hypocrisy which pretends to organize and govern individuals for their own good, but machine-guns them, or throws them into prison, when they try to escape from the exploitation and oppression imposed by their great-hearted directors and masters.

Enzo Martucci

2

Zoccoli [continues Sarafini] rightly says that the Stirnerian ethic is far removed from any possible application and merely has a sad speculative interest as the sophistical and delirious manifestation of a fortunately solitary thinker. Only if we returned to the life of the caveman could Stirner's teachings come true. You will have to agree also, Signor Martucci, that this is impossible.

I do not agree at all. I do not regard history as an infinite process. I believe that it must end one day. In spite of what philosophers from Aristotle onwards have said about the social tendency of man, history is nothing but the treatment of the organized and directed history of mankind, which has created conditions contrary to, and causing degeneration from, our natures. Either man will disappear, and with him history, or he will react healthily, destroy history and return to nature, gaining new strength as did Antacus when he touched the earth. Man is capable of evolution and improvement, but only by following his natural inclinations, not by suffocating them and transforming himself into a sheep or, worse still, a robot.

Education does not develop the individual, but depreciates or subdues him.

Education [says Callicles in Plato's Gorgias] takes the innate vigor from children and renders them weak. It makes them all alike and trains them for servile obedience. We take the best and strongest children and train them like lion cubs. We stun and fascinate them with our chattering and train them by teaching them that they have to be the same as all the others and that the beautiful and the good consist of this equality. But if there were a man who had sufficient force, he would shake off and break through, and escape from all this; he would trample underfoot all our formulas and spells and charms and all our laws which are against nature, then he who was our slave would reveal himself as the master.

But would civilization disappear? It would be better if it did. It also contributes to keeping man in shackles and it would be a good thing if it vanished. Besides, there does not exist only one civilization that presents a straight and evolutionary conception of history. As Spengler has so well shown, there have existed distinct and separate civilizations, which have all had a birth, a youth, a maturity, a decline, and a death. And all of these civilizations — except, perhaps, the Greek at the time of Pericles and the sophists — have tried to crush the originality and spontaneity of the natural individual, burdening his mind with dogmas and imposing laws on his conduct. One has done it in one way, another in another, and for different reasons, but all have agreed at least in this: the need to bridle the individual. Thus a new type of human being—who would be similar to Stirner's Unique or Nietzsche's Overman—would be unable to adapt himself to a civilization, but would want only to live in the free and luxuriant bosom of nature.

Despite this ethic which, according to Zoccoli, even the cannibal would reject, but which, according to Serafini, the caveman might accept, Stirner, "breaking his rigid individualism", endeavors to have it accepted by a social class: the proletariat. And for Zoccoli, Stirner does this in order

> to pay a necessary debt to the Left Hegelian school of thought from which he came, pointing out that as it was possible to use the individualist premise as a preparation for his own egoism, so it was also possible for the same consequences to find a more organic elaboration among the writers and successive movements of revolutionary communism.

It seems to Serafini that this is yet another contradiction in the author of The Ego and His Own, but in fact it is not. In 1845 the proletariat was not the organized, guided, well-paid and powerful proletariat of today, but a crowd of down-and-outs, unorganized and dissatisfied, who were chomping at the bit and in whom Stirner tried to arouse their egoism so that they could oppose it to that of their masters, and take from them their wealth. And this not in order to create a new society, but solely to satisfy the needs of the oppressed individual, who can, if necessary, resort to crime to obtain his own ends. Then he will become master of that which is his own—that is to say, that which he has the might to make his own. The State, which exists only to protect the interests of the property owner against those of the expropriated, would be abolished, but there must not be created a communist society in which everyone would belong to the organized collective and the individual would be unable to own anything, not even that which he is able to conquer and keep.

Enzo Martucci

When the proletarian shall really have founded his purposed 'society' [says Stirner] in which the interval between rich and poor is to be removed, then he will be a ragamuffin, for he will feel that it amounts to something to be a ragamuffin, and might lift 'Ragamuffin' to be an honorable form of address, just as the [French] Revolution did with the world 'Citizen'. Ragamuffin is his ideal, we are all to become ragamuffins.

This is the second robbery of the 'personal' in the interest of 'humanity'. Neither command nor property is left to the individual; the State took the former, society the latter.

Stirner, then, tends towards individualist anarchy and this always follows from his premise whether he is urging the individual to realize his value in relation to others, or the proletariat not to respect the property of the rich and to destroy the State, but not to create a communist society. He is against collective property, which is sacred and inviolable, and against individual property conceived as a right with the corresponding duty to respect it on the part of the destitute. He defends the egoistic property of the individual who has conquered and keeps it, and who no longer remains the owner when he allows others to take what he has gained.

Before Nietzsche announced the death of God, Stirner declared the end of the Sacred:

In crime the egoist has hitherto asserted himself and mocked at the sacred: the break with the sacred, or rather of the sacred, may become general. A revolution never returns, but a mighty, reckless, shameless, conscienceless, proud crime —does it not rumble in distant thunders, and do you not see how the sky grows presciently silent and gloomy?

The individual has to destroy in himself the ghosts which dominate him—god, Morality, Humanity, Society, etc.—and which impose duties, renunciations, and chains. He must understand that these ghosts do not represent any Superior Beings or Objective Entities, but are his own thoughts and creations projected outside and above him which he regards with timid reverence. But when he becomes aware of the real origin of these presumed supreme beings, and of the damage they cause—oppressing his spirit and impeding his actions—then he will repudiate them and, since they were his creations, destroy them. He becomes a self-owing individual.

This self-owner, who, in Zoccoli's opinion:

> acts with the aim of considering others as means, is faced with the actions —not associated and therefore not multiplied, it is true, but numerically additional —of all those others who invert the role obliterated by the absolute autonomy of all others.

This is not true. It would be if all the other self-owners simultaneously acted against me. But since they would not be organized this could not happen. They could only attack me singly or in small groups. Therefore I could defend myself, possibly with success. In more dangerous situations, I could resort to free alliances with others who, at that time, would benefit from supporting me, or in fighting my enemies. In brief, the struggle would not develop out of proportion and if I were overpowered today I could compete again tomorrow. And if I should die I would do so with the satisfaction of having tried to conquer a full and free life for myself. I would not have cowardly resigned myself to the chains of slavery and been content with the little others would allow me to have.

Today, in the civilized society Zoccoli so admires, if I do not want to adapt myself to a maimed and faded existence and rebel against it, I have all of organized mankind (a force far superior to mine and with far more formidable means) against me and, in spite of my heroism, would soon be crushed as were Jules Bonnet, Renzo Novatore, and Severino di Giovanni (illegalist anarchists who were killed by the State in France, Italy and Argentina).

I agree with Zoccoli about one thing only and that is where he recognized the perennial topicality of Stirnerian philosophy. In fact, after having established an ideological point of contact between Stirner and Hobbes, Zoccoli writes:

> While the doctrine of Hobbes is now recognized by scholars as evidence that cannot be ignored, so the doctrine of Stirner, while constructed on an erroneous and transcendental egoistic antinomy, as has been pointed out, still preserves a current importance and gives birth to many advocates.

Enzo Martucci

But not only bourgeois thinkers, like Zoccoli and Serafini, have stormed against Stirner. Revolutionary or pseudo-revolutionary thinkers have done the same.

Marx, in his book The German Ideology, spits venom at the author of The Ego and His Own. Gille, in his Outline of a Philosophy of Human Dignity, violently attacks Stirner as the theorist of an individualism which is not at all anarchist. Kropotkin tries to shatter him in a few words and believes he has won the game.

Following these great masters, who wanted to change the world, but had neither the courage nor the logic to persevere to the extreme limits at which Stirner arrived, the disciples parrot the judgments of their oracles. Some time ago a Sardinian who calls himself a follower of Malatesta wrote to me from America and asked

> Don't you find yourselves in contradiction, you and that German philosopher who call yourselves anarchists and predicate egoism without understanding that anarchy is only love for humanity and cannot be realized without general agreement?

I replied then, and I repeat now, that there is no contradiction if we call ourselves anarchists—that is, without government—and at the same time proclaim ourselves egoists. On the contrary, I want to be without government in order to be able to realize my egoism freely and completely, without being restrained and sanctioned by a sacred authority.

But what is egoism? It is an incoercible need that impels every living creature to provide for itself, to satisfy and enjoy itself, to avoid pain and preserve its life. The individual has no other end than his own ego, he cannot get out of his skin and all that he does he does for himself. He does nothing for the sake of others. When I deprive myself of my last piece of bread and give it to my neighbor who is hungry, I do so because the pain in my generous heart at his torment is less bearable than my hunger. If his agony did not pain me I would not give him my bread. Therefore I am an egoist, as is the sadist across the street who enjoys torturing animals and beating his wife and children.

The ascetic who renounces the pleasures of the flesh and consumes himself in penance, thinking that his temporary suffering will be compensated for by the eternal delights of heaven; the idealist who feels happy fighting for his ideal, which in reality exposes him to persecution and brings him misery; the ambitious man who uses every means and risks his life to conquer power; the miser who condemns himself to stinting and deprivation for the pleasure of hoarding money: the hedonist who, to enjoy the sensuality of the (of a) moment, squanders his money and spends his old age in poverty; the rebel who gets the satisfaction of striking at the master he hates and pays with his life or segregation in prison —these are egoists.

We are all egoists, even if the actions of one are different or opposed to those of another — the temperaments of individuals being as diverse as the passions that move them.

Altruism does not exist. It is no more than a Christian falsehood preserved and secularized by Auguste Comte with his religion of humanity when it seemed that the old faith was losing its power.

Therefore, to predicate egoism means also to arouse it in those in whom it has been made dormant by the theological and metaphysical narcotics administered by their masters. And when these slaves have rebelled and opposed their own egoism to the insatiable and hypocritical egoism of governments the situation will change. Then there will be no more resigned sheep on one side and commanding wolves on the other—only anarchism.

Anarchy, then, is not love for humanity but simply lack of government. In this absence of government and in the freedom that will come from it, those who feel love will love, and those who do not will not, and will maybe fight each other. We do not understand the motive that identifies freedom with universal harmony and would create one idyllic type of life in place of innumerable different ones. Therefore not even anarchy will produce a general agreement based on an absolute conformism but many free and relative agreements— unions of egoists—and many discords ranging from individual isolation to struggles between individuals and groups. This will be a return to nature, to the jungle, you say. Yes, but the natural jungle will be shown to be a thousand times preferable to the asphalt jungle.

However, the question between anarchists and archists has been badly stated from the beginning. In fact, we are not concerned with whether anarchy or archy can cement the best social relations, or bring about the most complete understanding and harmony between individuals. We try, instead, to discover which is the most useful for the realization and expression of the individual—who is the only existing reality. Is it anarchy, which offer me a free and

Enzo Martucci

perilous life, in which I might fall from one moment to another, but which allows me to affirm myself at least once? Is it archy, which guarantees me a controlled life in which I am confined and protected, but in which I can never live as I feel and will?

Which is preferable—intensity or duration?

Michelstaedter has said that preoccupation with tomorrow limits living.

I am for today. The sheep, even if they call themselves anarchists, long for tomorrow. And they die waiting for the sun of the future to rise.

To the anti-Stirnerism of the bourgeoisie, the Marxists and the libertarian socialist (Bakuninists, Kropotkinists, Malatestaians) must be contrasted the pseudo—Stirnerism of John Henry Mackay and E. Armand.

Pseudo-Stirnerism gives us a sweetened Stirner who tends towards the same end as the libertarian socialists—that is social harmony. But they do not think it can be achieved, as do the latter, by means of Bakunin's impulse to unity or Kropotkin's mutual aid, but rather through individual egoism. In order not to be attacked by others and have my life and freedom threatened, respect the life and freedom of others. it is not from love of my neighbors that I do not look for well-being in their suffering, but from personal interest.

But Stirner said nothing about this. He understood very well that in certain cases I cannot obtain the satisfaction of some of my needs without damaging the needs of others. If, for example, I want your woman, and you do not want to give her up or share her with me, I would have to snatch away, use violence, or try seduction, to make her love me and induce her to leave you. If I did not do this, if I suppressed my passion and left her with you, I would spare your sorrow, but would inflict it on myself. I would not put myself in danger of your revenge, but I should have to renounce an ardently desired joy. And so, going from one renunciation to another in order in not to clash with others, I would end by never having lived my life at all.

Therefore struggle is inevitable, and it is impossible to eliminate it from any kind of society or co-existence.

But there will be other cases in which my interests will correspond with those of my neighbors. Then I agree with them and add my force to theirs in order to achieve a common end. In this way is formed a union of egoists. But this union is based on a free agreement that can be cancelled at any time. Stirner explains it very clearly:

You bring into a union your whole power, your competence, and make yourself count; in a society you are employed, with your working power; in the former you live egoistically, in the latter humanly, that is, religiously, as a 'member of the body of this Lord', to a society you owe what you have, and are in duty bound to it, are possessed by 'social duties'; a union you utilize, and give it up undutifully and unfaithfully when you see no way to use it further. If a society is more than you, then it is more to you than yourself; a union is only your instrument, or the sword with which you sharpen and increase your natural force; the union exists for you and through you, the society conversely lays claim to you for itself and exists even without you; in short, the society is sacred, the union your own; the society consumes you, you consume the union.

Therefore the union of an egoist with other egoists is simply a temporary arrangement which can be quickly followed by disunion and struggle. It is not and cannot be a stable society based on the universal rule of "I respect you as long as you respect me".

E. Armand claimed outright that an individual could not break an agreement unilaterally —that is, leave an association without the consent of his fellow members. But this would mean that he would be dependent upon the others, he would be their slave, their property — just what Stirner did not want. To Armand's argument that I cannot abandon comrades who will not give me permission to do so because I must have regard for the pain my leaving would cause them, I have already replied that I do not concern myself with those who are not concerned with the pain they cause me by holding me back when I want to leave.

Certain authors confuse individualism with utilitarianism, Stirner with Bentham, the personal pleasure of the unique one with that of the majority or even of all. And they write works like Mackay's The Anarchists and Armand's L'initiation Individualiste Anarchiste which certainly do not contribute to the understanding of real Stirnerian thinking.

Enzo Martucci

8 FREE SPIRITS

The Eagle and The Serpent (1898–1927) was for a time published with the subtitle "A Journal of Free Spirits and for Spirits struggling to be Free." *The Eagle and The Serpent* favorably quotes Joseph A. Labadie in issue 18 (circa 1902), and later, in 1936, his son Laurance Labadie would use "A Journal for Free Spirits" as the subtitle for his own journal, *Discussion*. Laurance in turn was an influence on Mark A. Sullivan, who chose the same subtitle for his own gay individualist anarchist publication *The Storm* in 1976. In this same spirit, in this section, *Der Geist* collects "free spirits" too individualistic for other sections of our journal.

Peter Lamborn Wilson Has Passed **162**
Trevor Blake & Kevin I. Slaughter
2022

Hakim Bey: Real and Unreal. **163**
Mark Aelred Sullivan
2023

Vox Populi Vox Dei. **164**
Bonar Thompson
1930

Thompson at Rudolf Steiner Hall **167**
1941

Speakers' Corner Anthology **168**
Peace News
2023

Introducing "Among the Anarchists" **170**
Kevin I. Slaughter
2023

Among the Anarchists **171**
John Davidson
1896

The True Comarade **177**
E. Armand
1928

Is This What You Call "Living?" **178**
E. Armand
1912

The Thirteenth Paragraph **180**
E. Armand
1946

Greeves Fisher, A Sketch **185**
Christopher Draper
2016

Dominance vs. Egoism **191**
Peter McAlpine
1972

More Individualism **194**
Mark A. Sullivan
1975

Individualism and Property **196**
Mildred J. Loomis
1965

Why I am a Right-Wing Anarchist **198**
Robert Anton Wilson
1969

Opening and Closing the Dil Pickle **200**
Trevor Blake
2022

Christmas a Joke! **201**
Henry M. Tichenor
1914

"I" a poem **202**
Enrique Magon   1916

"I GO" a poem. **203**
Jack Jones   1927

A Letter to the Editors of *Freedom* **204**
Sidney E. Parker   1971

Enrico Arrigoni Bibliography **206**
Union of Egoists   2022

Photo of Benjamin R. Tucker **211**
Dorlys   (no date)

About the Editors **212**

Peter Lamborn Wilson Has Passed
Trevor Blake & Kevin I. Slaughter   2022

Peter Lamborn Wilson, also known as Hakim Bey, has passed. Peter was an enthusiast for *Der Geist*, the annual publication of The Union of Egoists. He volunteered to be an uncredited copy editor for several issues, for which we gave thanks and give thanks again.

I met Peter in Boston in 1987. He and I became correspondents. I published several of his essays in my zine *OVO* which were later collected in his book *T.A.Z.: The Temporary Autonomous Zone*. That's why he gives thanks to *OVO* in *T.A.Z.* My work appeared in two books he edited, *semiotext(e) USA* and *The Astral Convention* (the latter he gave me permission to reprint a very limited number of). I met Peter a second time a few years later in New York City, and after that a few phone calls, and after that letters with ever longer between them.

I still have the essays, zines and letters he sent me, many still uncollected. I still have the friends he introduced me to. But none of us have Peter any more.

TREVOR BLAKE

I was late to the egoist party by name, traveling to it from non-Anarchist origins. When Trevor and I began the work on the Union of Egoists project it was clear that Mr. Wilson was one of the few living bridges to the great figures of the egoist past. From his work with the Libertarian Book Club of New York City, his collaborations with Mark A. Sullivan and much more, I was pleased to have him as a correspondent in the last few years. It was with a great deal of pride that he took on a role as proofreader beginning with the second issue of our journal *Der Geist*, which he was quite fond of. He fell too ill to work on the fifth issue, but I was pleased to be able to send him a copy a few months ago with our best wishes. I sent him a Union of Egoists lapel pin, and tucked in a signed copy of his *Utopian Trace* he wrote a letter: "Thanx for lovely pin – send *GEIST* 3 galleys for proofreading if you wish!" I have only begun to explore the great deal of work he has now left behind, and I am proud that the Union of Egoists is, in some small way, part of that work.

KEVIN I. SLAUGHTER

Hakim Bey: Real and Unreal
Mark Aelred Sullivan
2023

Mark A. Sullivan founded and edited *The Storm,* an anarchist journal Peter Wilson became a co-editor of. "[We have] looked back to those whose lives exemplified anarchy in action: Emma Goldman, John Henry Mackay, Thoreau, the European Egoists, and Voltairine de Cleyre." *Hakim Bey: Real and Unreal* is published in October 2023 by mogtus-sanlux, available from UnderworldAmusements.com.

Hakim Bey: Real and Unreal is a cryptic book about a well-known cryptic writer by a less well-known cryptic writer. Th. Metzger writes with insider knowledge about his lifelong colleague and comrade, the now deceased Hakim Bey. Although he does acknowledge that Hakim Bey is a pen name for Peter Lamborn Wilson, except for one or two mentions of PLW, Metzger refers to Hakim rather than to Peter throughout.

HAKIM BEY
REAL AND UNREAL
Th. Metzger

Th. Metzger's memories of Hakim Bey are personal and subjective. Based on my own friendship with HB (over more or less the same period starting in the 1980s) they ring true. I cannot think of anything I knew or know about Hakim Bey that is at odds with the narrative presented by Th. Metzger. Those of us who knew HB could surely add to Metzger's memoirs—but our additions would most likely only serve to elaborate and reinforce what is recounted in *Hakim Bey: Real and Unreal.*

One matter that Metzger generously recounts is his shared in-depth interest with HB in mind-altering plants and substances—and a kind of "purple haze" seems to envelope the narrative.

To his credit, Metzger presents HB as well as himself more or less "warts and all." This is unusual for hagiography, although one could make a case that HB/PLW actually lived his life as "autohagiography". Indeed, it seems (even to Metzger) that "Hakim Bey was more or less a legend in his own mind—"a figment of his own imagination"—and that Peter Lamborn Wilson, the person behind the mask, thereby also remained out of grasp.

Vox Populi Vox Dei
Bonar Thompson

From *The Black Hat* Volume 1 Number 2 (October 1930).
Thompson writes about his time as a Conscientious Objector
prisoner, his disdain for the crowd and his praise for the individual in *Hyde Park Orator Illustrated* (Baltimore: Union of Egoists
2021).

Vox populi vox dei. It is more often the voice of the ventriloquist. The
war-lords, press-lords and money-lords pull the string and the figure
works.

"The people is a beast of muddy brain" wrote Campenella nearly
400 years ago "that knows not its own strength. Confused and stupe-
fied by bugbears vain, with its own hands it ties and gags itself; gives
itself death and war, for pence doled out by kings, from its own store."

Thomas Hardy wrote of "the pathetic people plodding on" while
G. K. Chesterton, in a famous poem, has written of "the secret people
of England who have not spoken yet."

For my part I think it extremely unlikely that they have any wish
to speak. They wish to be left alone.

Only on one occasion have I ever known the people of this country united in one cause for one purpose and speaking with one voice.
That was during the war of 1914 / 18. Out of a population of 47 millions there were 6,000 registered Conscientious Objectors, who refused to bow the knee to the Temple of Mars. These men were insult-
ed, abused, hounded into prison; many of them narrowly escaping
with their lives. In the great heart of the people there was no place
for them. They were outcasts in the land of their birth. The people
themselves were glad to offer their lives upon the altar of militarism.
They allowed themselves to be bullied, hectored, and lectured by the
Bottomleys and the Blatchfords, while the Press raved about "Roping
them in", "Rounding them up" and "Combing them out."

"Join the army and see the World" meant for thousands of them
joining the army and seeing the next world. One enthusiastic recruit-
ing orator, addressing a vast mob in Trafalgar Square, informed the
crowd that thousands of their comrades were dying in the trench-
es, and concluded by saying "Won't you join them?" Scores of young

men enrolled on the spot. Towards the end of the conflict there was such a shortage of fighting men that there was talk of calling up the Old Age Pensioners and combing out the Infant Schools, while outside Willesden Cemetery a huge placard bore the inscription "Wake up, England!"

At the close of the amazing business there was much bellowing and trumpeting about a "revolutionary situation" developing. Millions of men had grown so accustomed to killing that, finding themselves denied the "fruits of victory," they turned in a fury upon their respective governments, and for four or five years the world was troubled by insurrections, uprisings and abortive revolutions. In 1917 a vast change took place in Russia, where a handful of determined men led the masses from Czarism to the Dictatorship of Bolshevism. Since the death of Lenin, that country has been plodding its way steadily into Capitalism, and in 1930 we learn that it is fitted up with the latest modern improvements — a Secret Police, food queues, unemployment, and a rigorous prison system for those who wag their tongues too freely in favour of Freedom, that romantic fetish, of which, according to Mussolini, the world has grown sick.

The worship of machinery, mass production, and the general regimentation of the patient masses, point clearly to the growing development of Russia in a Capitalist direction. There are three classes in that happy land — the peasantry, who instead of praying to Saints, bow and cross themselves before a statue of Lenin, thus fortifying themselves for the toil which is their common lot on earth; the Civil Service bureaucrats of the Communist Party, who have naturally a vested interest in Communism and hold on like leeches to their jobs; and the Krassin Class, who visit Europe, dine with kings, quaff the champagne cup, and send their daughters to Oxford. The Revolution has devoured its children and sent into exile its most brilliant leader. The fallen Dictator is now begging for admission at the doors of every bourgeois country in Europe. Strange what an enthusiasm this man has developed for Liberty now that he is no longer in the saddle!

In the meantime the "pale, pathetic people" of Western Europe have plodded from one phase of government to another, without much appreciable improvement in their living or working conditions.

The rise of a new and independent party in England during post war years has not brought the rare and refreshing fruit as yet within the grasp of the masses. Most of the leaders are average men, and average men, however worthy they may be, are not the stuff from which great progressive schemes evolve.

All human advancement is the work of exceptional men, the thinkers and the doers of the world, who care nothing for rule or rote, precedent or custom, but go boldly on as their business and desires dictate. It is, perhaps, just as well that the people are never consulted in great affairs — except at Election times with tongue in cheek — for the people are never in favour of change. There is no reform, no progressive measure of any kind or description that has not been strongly opposed by what Ibsen called "the damned compact majority." The first man to carry an umbrella was laughed at as he passed through the streets; the first woman to ride a bicycle was hooted by the mob; the first motor-car was stoned; the first railway-train was denounced as an invention of Satan.

The extension of the school age; abolition of overtime; a shorter working day; have all been strenuously opposed by the majority of working people. Politically, their intelligence is below zero, and in matters calling for considered judgement, their opinion is of no value whatever.

Yet in spite of these grave defects, they are kindly, patient, and more free from snobbery than any other class. An atmosphere of friendliness prevails among them, so that one always feels at home in moving and mixing with them. Possessing little, they are the most hospitable people on earth. There cannot be anything fundamentally wrong with them. What they need is better education, more opportunities for travel, better conditions in which to live and work, so that they may develop those finer qualities which lie deep within their natures. No Government which fails to take these bold and drastic steps to grapple with this problem of the cultural and educational development of the people is worthy of support.

Thompson at Rudolf Steiner Hall

Handbill advertising a one-man entertainment by Bonar Thompson. This exceptionally rare bit of ephemera was laid into an early edition of Thompson's book, newly published in an expanded form by the Union of Egoists (*Hyde Park Orator Illustrated*, 2020).

RUDOLF STEINER HALL
UPPER BAKER STREET, N.W.1.

THURSDAY, 18TH SEPTEMBER 1941

A unique one-man entertainment will be given by

BONAR THOMPSON
The Famous Hyde Park Orator, Actor and Writer

> "He held the audience in his grip for three hours by sheer force of his oratorical and dramatic genius. Bonar Thompson is a wonderful personality of great gifts. His wit, courage, originality and amazing versatility deserve widespread acknowledgment."
> "*Daily Sketch.*"

> "The audience at the Fortune Theatre gave him an ovation that Ivor Novello might have envied."
> "*Daily Herald.*"

Mr. Thompson will, in response to many requests, present "The Ballad of Reading Gaol" by OSCAR WILDE.

Doors open 6-15.　　　**Curtain up at 6-30 prompt.**

MR. W. J. BROWN,
General Secretary of the Civil Service Clerical Association
WILL PRESIDE

TICKETS 2/6

Application for tickets should be made as early as possible to—

BONAR THOMPSON, 19 Arundel Gardens, W.11., or to Rudolf Steiner Hall. Padd. 8219.

Goodship & Co. Printers, 89, Praed Street, W.2.

Speakers' Corner Anthology
Peace News   2023

We are honored by Emily Johns' online review at *Peace News* of *Speakers' Corner Anthology*, edited by Jim Huggon and published by Union of Egoists. *Peace News* began publication in 1936, and this review appeared in February 2023. *Speakers' Corner Anthology* was published in May 2022 by Union of Egoists, available from UnderworldAmusements.com.

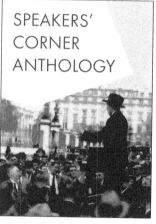

Peace News once organised an activist training in which the participants had to stand on a stepladder in Tavistock Square and deliver a speech to the passers-by.

It is a skill that people with a political opinion should have. But these days, few do.

Many quail at the simple political tool of door-knocking.

The *Speakers' Corner Anthology* is a collection of writings about the famous Tyburn corner of London's Hyde Park, by Marble Arch. There, since the mid-nineteenth century, speech-making has been tolerated by the park authorities (as long as no racing tips are shared). The park regulations are included in the book so one can see all the other categories of forbidden utterances.

The editor, Jim Huggon, was a speaker on the anarchist platform at Speakers' Corner for 18 years, after being invited up to 'have a go' by my father, John Rety.

Reading this book, I came to understand how standing on a ladder develops a speaker's quick wit and fearlessness, a closeness and connection with people, and a tolerance of diversity of opinion.

What an art! The writers in this anthology – the socialists, Christians, anarchists and communists – reveal that putting forward your ideas in public is not just about 'the gift of the gab', it is a studied and developed skill.

The anthology includes a fantastic piece of reportage by Karl Marx describing the energy and feistiness of the 1855 Sunday Trading Bill demonstrations, where participants harangued the toffs in Rotten Row for three hours ('Only English lungs are capable of such a feat'). Marx also analyses police strategy towards public demonstrations.

There are also humorous pieces by Bonar Thompson who, like others, made his living as an entertaining speaker – until 1926, when the park authorities banned passing the hat round. So many of the speakers had to have wit to counter hecklers – and humour to keep their crowd from drifting off to hear rival orators.

There is a beautiful piece by Methodist minister Donald Soper who spoke at the other public speaking pitch on Tower Hill (site of the other gallows in London). Soper writes on the personalities, eccentricities and friendships.

In all these writings, it is apparent that discourse, debate, heckling and profound disagreement over politics and religion did not lead to hatred. Which is very interesting when you compare this to the emotions generated by social media.

George Orwell writes about sellers of Freedom and Peace News being arrested in 1945 at Hyde Park and how the belief that the press is free was an overrated one, even though you could say anything you liked at Speakers' Corner.

On the other hand, Philip Sansom, an anarchist speaker from 1947 to 1960, is critical of the idea that free speech on this corner has any power at all. Rather, he argues, it is a form of kettling of expression into a safely-contained area.

Sansom points out that, during the postwar government, not a single Labour politician addressed the public at Speakers' Corner. They removed themselves safely from popular debate.

Despite his critique, I finished this engaging book with the understanding that public speaking helps you to think and that we should all be taking that risk and standing on the ladder in Tavistock Square.

Introducing "Among the Anarchists"
Kevin I. Slaughter
2023

The Scottish poet and novelist John Davidson wrote the following remarkable essay featuring an egoist anarchist at a Jewish anarchist meeting hall. Published in *Good Words* journal (1860-1910), written under the pseudonym "Menzies Macdonald," a name he also penned a few poems under.

Simon Cooke, Ph.d., summarized the monthly magazine on Victorian Web: "Devised by the Evangelical publisher...written by a variety of philanthropists, ministers of the church, pious versifiers and the converted, its texts are strictly traditional. ...Aimed at [religious] non-conformists, ...it gained currency as the classic 'fireside read', where it could be shared by adults and children, servants and masters."

A May 1893 letter to William Canton, a long time friend and General Manager of *Good Words*, excerpted in *The Review of English Studies*. In it Davidson remarked "I am glad the 'Anarchists' have passed muster." One presumes it was accepted for publication at that point, though it wasn't printed until the following year.

It was in 1893 his popular poetry collection *Fleet Street Eclogues* had just been published, and a collection of essays titled *Sentences and Essays*. It was three years later that "Among the Anarchists" was collected in the book *Miss Armstrong's and Other Circumstances*.

We have retained the British style quotation marks found in the original.

Davidson was one of the first Englishmen to promote the ideas of Friedrich Nietzche.

Among the Anarchists
John Davidson

'We can't go in there,' I said to the acquaintance who had persuaded me to visit a foreign club in Whitechapel.

It was cold; we were in a dark, narrow street; a drunken sailor lounged past us, grumbling at the universe; my companion had knocked at a low door, and upon its being opened I had recoiled from the noisome-looking entry ; the physical discomfort of dirt and evil smells seemed a price too dear for the new experience I had agreed to undergo.

'You can't go back now; it's quite clean inside,' replied my companion; he had visited the club more than once.

In we went, through an open court, and along a narrow, ill-lit passage—I shuddering and holding my breath, my companion whistling and unbuttoning his overcoat—and up some wooden steps to a landing, where a man, like an Italian, met us at the door of a little room. To him my companion said something, which he afterwards assured me was a greeting in Yeddish, the Hebrew-German patois. He also nodded to a woman who was selling ginger-beer to two fur-capped men ; she was a blonde Jewess, stout, pleasant-looking, neatly dressed, with a cigarette between her lips. Some more steps brought us into a small well-lit hall with a stage and curtain at one end. It was quite clean, the plain deal benches bearing still the marks of a recent scouring. On the walls were inscriptions in Hebrew letters; a large cartoon of the Chicago anarchists, Spies, Parsons, Linggard, Engel, and Fischer, who were executed a few years ago ; and an engraving of Lassalle—coarse ; almost a caricature; like a composite photograph of Peace, the murderer, and Lord Randolph Churchill. Some half-dozen men were hanging about the door—Polish Jews, my companion said.

We took seats near the middle of the room, and had not long to wait before it filled up. It was about five minutes to eight when we entered, and by eight o'clock there were nearly two hundred people assembled, men, women, and children; all of them clean, and tidily dressed; most of them remarkably contented and cheerful-looking; many of them with fresh complexions and bright eyes; handsome faces among both the men and the women. In height, the majority were under the average. They were nearly all Jews, I was told; dark, blonde, auburn; Russian, German, Polish, Italian ; by trade, mostly tailors and tailoresses. Conventional Jewish features were rare, however; among the men, not more than every sixth face could have been at once identified as Israelitish; there was less deviation in the women from the ordinary type.

They were all Nihilists, Anarchists, the extreme of social rebels. It was a club, but there was no smoking or beer-drinking ; they all seemed to know each other; families, groups of intimates, sat together talking and laughing; people moved about from seat to seat, or addressed each other across the room.

'Why, this is very tame,' I said to my companion. ' Where are your conspirators, your incendiaries, your regicides?'

He laughed, and bade me wait a little. Shortly a bell rang, and the curtain went up, discovering a chairman seated at a table. Behind him was a painted scene, and on either hand imitations of pillars and trees. He had a large brow, gray eyes, shaved cheeks, and a slight moustache. He was nattily dressed, authoritative-looking, evidently of more than average intelligence; only slightly Jewish in the cast of his features; liker an English than a foreign Jew. A carafe with water, a tumbler, and a handbell were on the table.

The chairman said a few words in Yeddish, which made his hearers laugh; then he announced a speaker and sat down.

A man left the audience, and entered on the scene from the right. He was rather tall, with very fair hair and fairer beard; mild, blue eyes; black clothes fitting him loosely; dishevelled, uplifted, the type of an enthusiast; not a Jew. He spoke in German, very rapidly. Only part of the audience understood him, but all were attentive. The speaker had no gesture, little motion of any kind, was diffident, self-conscious, but impressive. When he had spoken for a quarter of an hour, the chairman rang his bell. In less than five minutes the speaker wound up his address, and was at once questioned by two or three people successively. He gave satisfactory answers, and resumed his seat among the audience.

Then came a tall, chubby lad of seventeen or eighteen, whose appearance on the platform was hailed with cheers and laughter. He was not a buffoon, however; the audience were laughing at the recollection of humorous sayings of the youthful orator and in anticipation of fresh witticisms. He spoke slowly, smoothly, without effort, and the Yeddish had a mellow sound in his clear rich voice. Soon he had everybody shaking with laughter ; they laughed quietly lest they should miss a single point. Suddenly the mirth died down, faces grew pale, and tears came into the eyes of women. As suddenly the laughter burst out again, unrestrained this time, crackling and spluttering among the tears. The speaker alone seemed unmoved. It was a most remarkable display in a mere boy of the highest oratorical power.

The third and last speaker was a Polish Jew – a little dark man with a thin, pleasant enough face, and burning black eyes. He was received demonstratively, and plunged at once into a tirade – an indictment of Capitalism, or of Society in general, doubtless. He drove his charges home with clenched hands and a pouring delivery, which had the effect of a shower-bath on the audience, leaving them breathless and glowing all over.

After the speeches the chairman stepped down from the platform, and a conversazione began, everybody smiling and in the best of humour. Cigarettes, cigars, and a few pipes were now lit ; and the women and children ate cakes and drank lemonade.

'Well?' queried my companion.

'I am much amazed and amused,' I said.

'Do you know what it reminds me of?'

'A Young Men's Mutual Improvement Society?'

'Very nearly. To me this meeting of Anarchists is exactly like a church soireé. There is, apparently, the same respectability, the same easy, simmering excitement, the same perfect confidence in the absolute uprightness of their purpose in meeting together. I should say that this club is no more dangerous to the State than a Missionhall.'

'I am not so sure about the danger,' replied my companion, ' but

I agree with the rest of what you say. Their political creed is the religion of these people; and as human nature is identical everywhere, their weekly meetings present the same phenomena as the weekly meetings of any other body of people united in doctrine. I confess that it has been somewhat tame to-night. I have seen hot debates, heard hoarse cries, and watched stealthy hands groping for revolvers and knives.'

'What! to fight among themselves?'

'Oh, no! Excited almost to the point of running amuck.'

'Come, now,' I said, 'how do you know that there are revolvers and knives here?'

My companion answered rather evasively. He had interpreted certain actions to mean the clutching of weapons; but I gathered that he had never seen either a knife or a revolver within the walls of this club.

Families, groups, sweethearts, and individuals began to leave; by half-past nine the hall was cleared. My companion introduced me, in the anteroom, to the chairman, the speakers, and several other Anarchists ; and I started a conversation with the crude announcement 'that popular common- sense which regards Anarchism as synonymous with violence and dynamite is as right as ever it was.'

'Ah!' said the enthusiast, who spoke English correctly, and with little accent, 'that is just what Society says, " No compromise;" and that is what we say.'

'But dynamite is a compromise,' I rejoined. 'War in any form is, and always has been, a compromise: both parties, afraid of being put in the wrong by the "no compromise" of impartial arbitration, fly to arms.'

A tolerant smile was the only reply the enthusiast deigned to give to my paradox.

'Everyting,' said the fiery Polish Jew, 'ees gompromyce. Ze woarld ees a gompromyce between ze inanity and someting.'

The enthusiast rejoined in Yeddish. It seemed to me that he was explaining to the Polish Jew his own meaning: I wish he had explained it to me. Then he went on in English, 'Yes, everything is a compromise. Life itself is the only evil, and all our organizations and schemes are a compromise, or an attempted compromise, with it. I refer everything to the two poles, positive and negative. The negative is the supreme unattainable good ; the positive is the supreme ever-present evil. If we live we compromise; "no compromise" would be a destruction of all life in order to attain the unattainable.'

'Then you admit that the true doctrine of the Anarchists is one of destruction?'

'I do. Hegel marks the culminating point of the purely theoretic side of modern culture ; therefore we have arrived precisely at the point where the necessary dissolution of that culture ought to begin.'

'Why, then, you are a Nihilist,' said my companion.

'If you like. I would prefer, however, to be called an Annihilist. I have never quite understood how the word Nihilist got its vogue. We don't believe in nothing; on the contrary, we are intoxicated with belief in everything conceivable, and wish to annihilate it.'

This the enthusiast said with nonchalant gravity, as if it were even simpler to organise a revolution for the annihilation of humanity than for the overthrow of a government.

'But would you not be content with change?' I asked.

'For my part, I believe change is impossible. The form may alter, has altered, again and again; but you will always have dominant and serving classes, always rich and poor.'

At this a tall, red-bearded German, who spoke good English, burst in with a disclaimer.

'No, no!' he cried;' you misrepresent Anarchism or, at least, you may cause this gentleman to misunderstand it. Anarchism is the individual revolution as distinct from the collective revolution. The collective revolution is impossible, because we exist, not as a community, but only as individuals.

You see? There is nothing above me, nothing without me, nothing within me, greater than myself. I do not submit myself to my spirit, mind you. My spirit, like my flesh, is only one of my qualities; the individual is more than soul and body.'

'Well, now, what is the individual?' asked my companion.

'The individual, the ego!' replied the German. 'There are no words to define it; it is unsayable; it cannot be named; it is perfect; every individual is every instant exactly what he can be, and nothing more or less. I know of nothing that can impose duty on me. I do not consider myself as an individual among other individuals, but as the only individuality which exists. All things men and so-called property are my goods and chattels in proportion as my force allows me to appropriate them.'

The enthusiast attempted an interruption at this point in the German's harangue, but the latter bore him down.

'You see, it is simply freedom,' he said, 'and one is free in proportion as one is strong ; there is no liberty except what you take. The State, Religion, Humanitarianism, Socialism all that disappears before the Sovereign ME. Truth itself signifies nothing. Thoughts are the creatures of the individual; they are not themselves the individual. I say that to believe in a truth, in any truth, is to abdicate the individual. Thus we are all fighting against each other, and every weapon is allowable—poison, infernal machines, because all that is required to become immediately endowed with an inalienable right to have a thing is that one should desire to possess it.'

'Would it not be wise, then,' I asked, 'in an individual holding your opinions, to keep them to himself? For his own sake, I mean; he will have a better chance of securing what he wants if he alone acts on his "no principle." You are too benevolent; you arm every one against you if you tell the world that you have taken for your creed the negation of the decalogue.'

'Error!' said the red-haired German coolly. It is not for love of men, still less for love of truth, that I express my thoughts, but for my own pleasure exclusively. I speak because I have a voice, and I address you because you have ears for which my voice was intended.'

'Let me speak now,' said the chairman.'I should like this gentleman to see that there are as many kinds of Anarchism as there are men—me, for example. I want to be a tyrant; to relieve the world of all moral clogs and world-old prejudices; to be the anarch, and found a new religion and a new legislative system for my own glory.'

The chairman's brief declaration elicited no surprise from his companions, and I received it as a matter of course.

'I understand Anarchism now,' I said; 'it is simply, Every man his own god.'

'Precisely,' said the enthusiast.

'Of course you are all wrong,' said my companion. 'Don't you see that Anarchism is the exaggeration of the idea of Liberty, just as Socialism is the exaggeration of the idea of Equality? Both have parted company with each other, and with Fraternity. In my opinion, Society is quite healthy, although its constitution may be run down, largely the result, I should say, of a dissipation in Liberty and Equality. You have divorced these two ideas from Fraternity, without which they cannot hold water. Did nobody ever say to you, "Little children, love one another"? Liberty, Equality, Fraternity! For the first two we want to substitute Duty and Reverence. Fraternity means Charity.'

Those who understood him smiled tolerantly and went for their hats; they were not there to listen. They wished us 'Goodnight ' frankly and cheerily, and my companion and I took our departure.

Free Spirits

The True Comarade

E. Armand

Translated from *"Le vrai camarade"* in Armand's journal *L'en dehors* number 137 (July 1928).

Worthy, you are far too dignified to bear the thought that someone
    might have given more than you have received—
or that the one who gives to you might suspect that they have re-
    ceived less than their contribution—
I know well that you will say, "Fair is fair..."—
and that you consider yourself "an egoist among the egoists"—
But egoist, you are much too egoist—
to admit that, being able to give pleasure to someone in your world—
you would refuse yourself the delight of doing so—
I am well aware that you speak constantly of "reciprocity"—
but you never believe you have paid enough for a smile, reimbursed a
    kind word, acquitted a sign of sympathy—
you are much too individual to accept that, in their relations with
    you, that one of your own should have reason to fear that they
    have not been paid in return—
You insist, to all who will listen, that you are only bound by the terms
    of the contract that you have concluded with one of your own—
but I have seen you, a thousand times, torment yourself, wrack your
    brain, asking yourself—
if you have exactly fulfilled your obligations—
"exactly"—
that is, exactly as intended by the one who had contracted with you—
at the moment when you signed it—
You are much too "unique," too proud—
to not exhaust, to the utmost extreme—
the capacity to give, to make and to satisfy—
in order not to leave, hands empty and their desire unfulfilled, the
    one of your own who reached out to you—
imagining you rich in possibilities...

Is This What You Call "Living?"
E. Armand
1912

From *Hors du Troupeau* ("Outside the Crowd") (1912).

Get up at dawn. Running or using any means of rapid locomotion. Go to "work." That is, shut up in a room–spacious or confined, airy or airless. Sitting in front of a typewriter, tapping away transcribing letters of which we would not send half if we had to write them by hand. Or, working to shape always the same parts from a machine. Or, yet again, not getting away more than a short distance from equipment that has to be operated or be monitored. Or, finally, mechanically, automatically, standing in front of a loom, repeating the same gestures, making the same movements. And that for hours and hours on end without any distraction, without any change in the environment. Everyday;
   Is this what you call "living"?

Produce! Produce again!! Always produce!!! Like yesterday, like the day before yesterday. Like tomorrow–unless you are sick or dead. Produce? Things that seem useless but you are forbidden to discuss their superfluity. Complex objects of which only a tiny part is in the hands while we never know the whole of the manufacturing process. Produce? Without knowing the destination of the product. Without being able to refuse to produce for whom you do not like. Without being able to show individual initiative. Produce quickly, rapidly. To be a stimulated tool prodded, jostled, and exhausted until nothing can be extracted from it, only a cent of profit;
   Is this what you call "living"?

Leave early in the morning hunting for customers. Pursue, track down the interested buyer. Jumping from Métro to a taxi, a taxi-car to a bus, a bus to an electric tram. Unless it's in a muddy river. Make fifty visits a day. Using his saliva to hawk merchandise. Shouting, inconsiderate of others. Come home in the late evening, burdened, jaded, worried, making everyone unhappy, emptied of all inner life, of all drive towards a better, moral being;
   Is this what you call "living"?

Languish between the four walls of a cell. To feel, as the accused, the unknown of the future separating you from those whom you love, either by affection or by affiliation. Sentenced to feel that your life is escaping you, that you can do nothing to determine it. And that for months, for years. No longer able to struggle. To be no more than a number, a play-thing, a rag, an object stamped, watched, overseen and used. All this far beyond the equivalence of the committed offense;

Is this what you call "living"?

Wear a uniform. For one, two, three years, repeating the actions of a murderer. In full bloom of youth, in full explosion of manhood, locking oneself in large buildings from where you exit and return only at fixed hours. Eat, walk, wake up–to do–everything and nothing–at a set time. All this to learn how to handle devices taking life away from strangers. Expecting to fall one day, struck by some bullet from out of sight, shot by unknown hands. To be trained to perish–or to make others perish. An asset, a pawn, in the hands of the Privileged, the Powerful, the Monopolists, the Hoarders. While you are neither privileged nor powerful nor own anything;

Is this what you call "living?"

Not being able to learn, love, keep to yourself, or wander at will. Having to stay shut in when the sun shines or the flowers of the forest unfurl. Unable to go South when the wind is freezing and the snow up against our windows. Or to the North when the heat simmers and grass burns in fields. Always, everywhere, laws, borders, conventions, the rural police, morals, conventions, judges, factories, prisons, barracks, and men in uniform protecting, maintaining, or defending an order of things hindering the expansion of the individual;

Is this what you call "living?"

O lover of "the intense life," fawners over "progress," peddlers of the chariot wheels of civilization.

I call this stagnation. I call it death.

The Thirteenth Paragraph
E. Armand

From *L'Unique* (April 9, 1946).

The Thirteenth Paragraph
(Account of a Nightmare)

A large room, a basement or cemented cellar. Behind a long rectangular oak table, three characters are seated; in the middle, a woman, to her right and left, a man. Due to the positioning of the lampshade on the lamp placed in the center, which casts the light onto the surface of the table, their features are only vaguely distinguishable. At a distance of three or four meters from the table, a wooden bench. The walls are bare. There are no other furnishings in the room.

The woman sitting in the middle (addressing the two men on either side of her, while she finishes leafing through an open file in front of her). - You are familiar with the file.

The man sitting on the right.—I have thoroughly examined it.

The man sitting on the left.—I have studied it carefully.

The woman sitting in the middle.—We only have to wait now.

(Hardly has she spoken these words when a door opens in the back wall. Emerging from the shadows, a masked man is seen, leading a blindfolded woman. Without uttering a word, he guides her to the bench and removes her blindfold. Mechanically, she collapses onto the bench. The man withdraws to the back of the room.)

The woman sitting on the bench.—What do you want from me? Who are you?

The woman sitting in the middle.—We are Paul's friends.

The woman sitting on the bench.—I don't know you.

The woman sitting in the middle.—That doesn't matter. But do you know who Paul was?

The woman sitting on the bench.—Paul, poor Paul (her voice trembles). Of course, I know him... I knew him.

The woman sitting in the middle.—If what we know is correct, you were not unaware that Paul was affiliated with an association called "Few, but Certain"?

The woman sitting on the bench.—Indeed, he mentioned it to me. But I am not part of your association. Once again, what do you want from me?

The woman sitting in the middle.—You will soon find out. The thirteenth paragraph of the oaths that bind us together is formulated as follows: "If any of us were to suffer harm or damage from another, regardless of who it may be, we swear to provide them with unconditional aid and support until they have obtained proportional reparation for the harm caused. If any of us were to suffer emotionally or materially because of another, regardless of who it may be, we swear to offer them unconditional aid and support until they have obtained from the perpetrator of the inflicted suffering either reparation or healing. If such harm or damage were to result in the death of any of us, we swear to seek vengeance for it, regardless of the consequences." Did you also not know about this?

The woman sitting on the bench.—I knew he was proud to belong to your association. He often told me that associating with like-minded individuals increased personal strength and multiplied individual power. He frequently spoke to me about the principle that drove you: "One for all, all for one." I knew you were bound to each other by strict oaths, but I was unaware of their exact nature. I don't see where you're going with all of this. What does it have to do with me?

The woman sitting in the middle (while leafing through the file in front of her).—Paul was your friend. He loved you, but from what we know, you did not return the love he felt for you. It caused him immense suffering. However, you agreed to be loved by him. Is that correct?

The woman sitting on the bench.—I had pity for him.

The man sitting on the right.—Pity is a sign of a generous soul, but for it to be effective, it cannot stop halfway; otherwise, it only exacerbates the wound it seeks to heal.

The man sitting on the left.—Pity is superior to love. Being loved out of pity does not diminish the one who accepts it, because of the richness of heart it reveals in the one who loves in such a way. Not everyone is capable of loving out of pity.

The woman sitting in the middle.—Nevertheless, he harbored for you a very intense, deep, and sincere love. If our information is correct, he had declared to you that his last card was dependent on this love. Is that correct?

The woman sitting on the bench.—Yes.

The woman sitting in the middle.—Although the lack of reciprocity on your part tormented him, he did not complain to us, as paragraph XIII provided him the opportunity to do so. After all, the nature of your relationship does not concern us. It was your affair. One day, the justice of men sent Paul to prison for two years. A few days after his conviction, you stopped giving him any sign of life. He wrote to you, begged you to give him the reasons for your silence: you remained silent. We know that your silence multiplied his pain of feeling cut off from active life. He spent twenty-four months in the grip of indescribable emotional agony. Upon his release, he took the first train and went to you to seek clarification about your behavior. It seems that he found you in the arms of another, literally speaking. He immediately returned to the hotel room he had rented in the meantime. He locked himself in there. An hour later, a gunshot was heard. It didn't take long to locate its source. The door to the room was forced open, and Paul was found lying on his small bed, bathed in his own blood. He had shot himself in the heart and had not missed. Is all of this correct?

The woman sitting on the bench.—Yes, but...

The woman sitting in the middle.—That's not all. On the table in that hotel room, there was a letter addressed to us. Not long, just a few lines. Here it is: "The one I loved failed in her promise. It's more than I can bear. I prefer to take my own life, but as I die, I appeal to paragraph XIII; avenge me."

The woman sitting on the bench.—What promise?

The woman sitting in the middle.—In a letter from your hand, attached to the one he sent us, there is a passage underlined by him: "To prove to you how much I appreciate the sincerity and depth of your feelings towards me, I can promise you that, as long as you live, I will never be with another man." Is that correct?

The woman sitting on the bench.—Yes, I wrote that. He complained about my coldness, my hardness, my cruelty, my insensitivity. I wanted to ease his pain, soften his suffering.

The woman sitting in the middle.—You are thirty years old. At your age, you are no longer a little girl. We have among us women who are ten years younger than you, and we entrust them with perilous missions where they risk their lives at any moment. What they have to accomplish is not always to their liking, but not a single one of them has ever failed in her oath. A promise made is a promise kept. That's our moral code.

The woman sitting on the bench.—Wasn't I free to release myself from my promise?

The woman sitting in the middle.—No, not according to our

beliefs, without agreeing upon it with the one to whom it bound you. We do not accept unilateral termination of the pact. Just as one does not break a commitment made, except in the case of mutual consent. On this matter, we do not compromise. You are even more guilty in regards to Paul because, in the situation imposed on him, he could neither object, defend himself, nor verbally present any argument against you...

The man sitting on the right.—The consequences of your broken promise have deprived us of Paul's friendship. He was dear to us. For us, friendship is sacred. Whoever takes away one of our friends commits a crime.

The woman sitting on the bench.—I had nothing to do with the situation imposed on Paul. What's done is done; I cannot undo it. I value my own freedom above any promises I could have made...

The man sitting on the left. - Your freedom ends where the consequences of its exercise bring grief to a circle that had never caused you any harm. No, you were not free, through your perjury, to take Paul away from our friendship.

The man sitting on the right.—You confuse freedom with license. License is superficial; it changes with time and circumstances; it wears the mask of all kinds of successive and contradictory influences; it veers with every wind; it lacks responsibility. Freedom, on the other hand, is based on responsibility; it is founded on reason and reins in appetites; it is constancy and not whim, not bent before circumstances but constantly in a state of perpetual defense against their grip.

The woman sitting in the middle.—No doubt, in the final analysis, everyone is free to unilaterally release themselves from a promise, but it is at their own risk. That is why you are here, before us, sitting on this bench. And the thought didn't occur to you to end your own life?

The woman sitting on the bench.—I never imagined that Paul would commit suicide. I had no idea that his love for me was so intense. When I learned the news of his death, I was shocked. I am sorry, devastated, but what can I do? Taking my own life wouldn't bring him back!

The woman sitting in the middle.—Certainly not, but it would have spared us the trouble. Do you understand that Paul was our friend and that, among us, friendship is a matter of life and death? Do you understand that, because of your perjury, each one of us was pushed into despair? Do you understand that it's not just the blood in which his body was bathed that cries out for vengeance, but it's as if the blood in which all our bodies are immersed is pleading for revenge? One for all, all for one. We hold you accountable for Paul's death.

The woman sitting on the bench.—How could I have known that Paul would come to this extreme?

The woman sitting in the middle.—I repeat, you are no longer a little girl to act without caring about the near or distant consequences of your actions. We know that you were fully aware of the strength of the love that Paul had for you.

The woman sitting on the bench.—I repeat to you that what is done is done, and we cannot go back on the past, no matter how immediate it may be. If we always had to think about the consequences of our actions, we would never undertake anything.

The woman sitting in the middle.—That is not our moral code. Do you have anything else to add in your defense?

The woman sitting on the bench.—In my defense? Am I before judges?

The woman sitting in the middle.—Yes, you are. Since Paul, our friend, claiming paragraph XIII, asked us to avenge him, we accuse you: first, of being the cause of his suicide, due to your broken promise; second, of taking him away from our friendship. We declare you doubly guilty. As a punishment for your crimes, I condemn you to death... (addressing the man sitting on the right)—And you?

The man sitting on the right.—To death.

The woman sitting in the middle (addressing the man sitting on the left).—And you?

The man sitting on the left.—To death.

The woman sitting in the middle (to the woman sitting on the bench).—You may leave.

(The woman sitting on the bench stands up, walks towards the door that has just opened. She walks as if in a daze. The masked man follows her at a distance of two or three steps. The door closes. Moments pass in silence, then the sound of a gunshot is heard.

The woman sitting in the middle.—Our friend Paul is avenged. Justice has been served!

October 15, 1943

Greeves Fisher, A Sketch
Christopher Draper

From *Northern Voices* No. 10 (October 2016), with kind permission of Christopher Draper. Fischer was a regular contributor to Benjamin R. Tucker's journal *Liberty* (1881), a subscriber to *The Eagle and The Serpent* (1898), and was a member of the Legitimation League. A fellow member of that "free love" organization was John Badcock Jr., and one of his lectures to the group was published under a pseudonym in the pamphlet *For Love and Money*. This rare booklet was reprinted as an issue of Stand Alone (2016). Wendy McElroy, in a talk delivered at the Ludwig von Mises Institute in 2000, referred to Greevz as "among the best voices on economics" of contemporary British individualist anarchists.

Leedz Anarkyst—Greevz Fysher (1845-1931)

Greevz was one of England's most original yet least known pioneering anarchists. From the economy to the alphabet, if there was a conventional system, Greevz had an alternative!

A Marriage Made in Heaven—and Leeds

Born John Greeves Fisher in Youghal, Ireland on 9 September 1845, Greevz preferred the phonetic form of his name in line with his scheme for spelling reform. Initially employed as an ironmongers assistant in Dublin, in 1877 Greevz moved to Wetherby, Yorkshire to partner his cousin in his Leeds "Kingfisher" engineering business. After his first wife died, in 1879, Greevz lived with her widowed sister, Charlotte Rowntree. Although both shared a Quaker upbringing Greevz had since progressed through scepticism to full-blown atheism and Charlotte wasn't amused. In 1884 Daniel Pickard told the Leeds Quaker congregation that, "We much regret to have to inform the Monthly Meeting that John G. Fisher has been for some time past an acknowledged disbeliever on the fundamental truths of the Christian religion". Charlotte moved to America and in September 1887 at Leeds Register Office, Greevz married the love of his life, Marie Clapham.

Klever and Kreativ

Marie shared and encouraged Greevz' iconoclasm and the joyful inventiveness that had already borne fruit. In 1884 Greevz had marketed, "Fisher's Nonpareil Perpetual Kalendar" and the following year published, "Spelling Reform in Three Stages". He then developed an improved device for producing reading material for the blind. Marketed as the "Kingfisher Braille Printer" and adopted by Liverpool blind school it was only a modest success.

By then his cousin had left the engineering business, making Greevz sole proprietor. Greevz re-focussed the business onto developing lubricants for industry. In 1883 he came up with "ACME" a unique, soap-based grease that proved invaluable.

In 1886 Greevz first mounted the pulpit to rail against religion and April found him at Sheffield's "Hall of Science" delivering a couple of characteristic sermons. In the afternoon he spoke on, "Spiritualism a Delusion" and in the evening, rhetorically reassured listeners, "Has a Dying Atheist Anything to Fear?"

Cheeky Lady

Marie Fisher was a secularist freethinker in her own right and according to her son, "as a young country girl she used to tramp the 12 miles to attend the meetings of Charles Bradlaugh". Greevz and Marie first met at one of these secularist meetings and the couple's selection of names for their 5 children signals their influences and advertises their radicalism;

- Auberon Herbert (1888-1932) – named after the individualist anarchist
- Wordsworth Donisthorpe (1889-1950) – another English anarchist
- Constance Naden (1891-1984) – female poet and philosopher
- Spencer Darwin (1893-1968) – libertarian philosopher and discoverer of evolution
- Hypatia Ingersoll (1899-1977) – philosopher martyred by Church & an American libertarian

Marie didn't confine her interests to the home, and every Wednesday attended educational classes at Leeds' Mechanics' Institute. When local magistrates refused to accept affirmation as an alternative to "swearing on the bible", she doggedly pursued the issue through the press. In 1904 she travelled to the Rome International

Freethought Congress as a delegate of the British Secular League and relished the perceived insult to Catholicism in the pages of "The Truthseeker", "The Pope thinks that the gates of hell cannot prevail against the Church but he sees rationalism forcibly pronouncing itself within earshot of the Vatican. He admits he is grieved; possibly he trembles."

Marie was an active member of the local Astronomical, Philosophical, Geological and Yorkshire Naturalists' Societies and, in 1923 was elected as the first female president of the Leeds Philatelic Society. She was a militant feminist and active suffragette and in 1920 Marie wrote to the press encouraging Leeds ladies to light up in cinemas after seeing notices permitting men to smoke but prohibiting women.

Freethought to FREEDOM

Encouraged by Marie's own iconoclasm it wasn't long before Greevz' Freethought widened out into political activism. In 1888 he supported the local strike of Jewish tailors and at the Clarendon Buildings denounced, "Starvation in the Midst of Plenty". He also began a six year campaign for election onto local School Boards. Greevz opposed the growing State control of education and was determined to derail the process in Leeds but was never elected.

Even within anarchism, Greevz adopted an advanced position on children. In an article entitled, "Children as Chattels", he argued against Benjamin Tucker, in Tucker's journal, "Liberty", that parents don't own their children. They certainly owe them a duty of care but children own themselves and should be respected as individuals from the start. Greevz had real insight into libertarian learning and as well as generally campaigning against state control of schools he also specifically opposed the abstract curriculum that came with it. In 1889 he argued in, "The Revolutionary Review", "Keeping children from manipulating tangible objects and forcing them to occupy themselves almost wholly with symbols is a total reversal of the natural order of intellectual growth."

Anarchism or Communism

Greevz remained forever sceptical of the millennarial promises of Communists. Although he subscribed to the Anarchist-Communist journal "Freedom" he objected to Kropotkin's assurances that history was inevitably moving in the direction of communism. History shows Greevz was right to be sceptical. Whilst Kropotkin's observations on mutual aid were a useful corrective to the excesses of social Darwinism, "Freedom" continued to over-egg the pudding and exaggerate revolutionary prospects. Greevz was one of a small group of English anarchists who fought against State control and argued for voluntary cooperation yet refused to accept that "Anarchist-Communism" could square the circle. He was presciently aware of the group-think dangers inherent in all forms of Communism.

From its 1898 inception, Greevz subscribed to the Egoist journal *The Eagle and the Serpent* (E&S) from and enthusiastically responded to its editor's appeal for supporters to form affinity groups – "Egoist Coteries", "Nietzsche Clubs", "Myself Societies" – by proposing himself as Leeds coordinator of an "Egoist Lending Library". Once established, E&S advertised this network as "Egoist Universities", which grew to include Scottish anarchist William Duff as its Glasgow representative. Unfortunately the scheme never operated effectively and after publishing nineteen iconoclastic editions the journal finally ceased publication in 1903.

Natural Order

After anarchism and family-life, Greevz loved cycling. He'd started in Ireland on a boneshaker with wooden wheels and iron tyres but had still managed journeys of over 100 miles. In later life he rode a variety of fairly modern machines and into his eighties he rode almost every day. Greevz' cycling exploits featured regularly in "The Leeds Mercury" where he revealed his recipe for a long and active life, "I consume a fair amount of home-made lemonade" and "I make my own porridge".

Greevz was also keen on natural history, a respected member of several local societies, in 1930 he was elected President of the Yorkshire Naturalist's Union. His non-political lecture repertoire included;

"Some Curious Habits of the Indian Wasps"
"The Sinistral Form of Limnaea Peregra"
"The Structure and Habits of the Crayfish"

In later years Greevz combined an interest in wildlife with a passion for cycling and indulging his eccentricity he was regularly spotted cycling around Leeds with a pet jackdaw perched on his shoulder!

Yorkshire Anarchy

Greevz was a much loved local character but was also a serious, inventive owner of a small, successful business employing around 30 people. As a Proudhonian advocate of small scale enterprise he never contemplated converting "Kingfisher" into a workers' co-op but according to a former employee writing in the "Yorkshire Post", "We all had a real affection for him".

Greevz followed up the great success of his, "Kingfisher Acme Lubricant" with the invention and production of an original,"Screw Plunger Automatic Lubricator" which continues, in modified form, in production today. Interestingly, for many years Greevz employed Leonard Hall, a pioneering Manchester socialist as Kingfisher's sales agent. Greevz' monetary theories were then critically examined in one of Hall's political tracts, "Which Way? Root Remedies & Free Socialism Versus Collectivist Quackery and Glorified Pauperism".

Whatever folks thought of his politics the business thrived and continues today, still under family ownership. Greevz updated, patent grease fittings, have over the years been installed in vehicles ranging from Volvo cars through the European Airbus to NASA's space shuttle transporter.

Catalogue of Surgical Specialities

Greevz was a keen analyst of the role money and markets play in capitalist society but in contrast to the Anarchist-Communists he wasn't satisfied that problems of distribution and exchange would evaporate if capitalism were destroyed. The debates appear abstract and protracted but the problem is real enough.

Greevz and Marie also enthusiastically attacked traditional constraints on sexual relations and reproduction. They didn't merely campaign for women's right to limit family size but bravely also advertised and supplied contraceptives in an age that was outraged. In the 1890's they freely supplied interested parties with their "Malthusian Catalogue of Domestic & Surgical Specialities". Greeves also campaigned against the labelling of children as "Bastards" and organised for the repeal of oppressive legislation as President of the "Legitimation League".

Unlike Kropotkin, Greevz didn't promise heaven on earth. Although he disagreed with Benjamin Tucker on some of the finer points they shared the same basic practical anarchist approach; "There are some troubles from which mankind can never escape...They (the anarchists) have never claimed that liberty will bring perfection;

they simply say that its results are vastly preferable to those that follow from authority...As a choice of blessings, liberty is the greater; as a choice of evils, liberty is the smaller. Then liberty always says the Anarchist. No use of force except against the invader..."

In the 1880's Greevz campaigned against granting the Post Office a monopoly over telegram delivery. In the 1890's he argued against doctors claiming immunity from public scrutiny as he rejected all forms of professional cartel, "Classes based upon special privileges are a danger to the public liberty".

Throughout his long life Greevz continued to resist authority and speak up for the dispossessed. Through the pages of "Liberty" he continued to argue for the liberation of Ireland but unlike the Fenians he didn't want an Independent Irish State, he proposed "No Government for Ireland!" Aged 83, he wrote to the "Yorkshire Post" criticising the local authority who'd demolished the homes of the Beeston Community of Tolstoyan anarchists because they refused to fully comply with the Council's petty demands.

Ashes to Ashes

Celebrating Greevz, long involvement in civic life, in September 1925 the "Yorkshire Post" observed, "Mr Greevz Fisher, head of the firm of Kingfisher (Ltd) lubricators and oil merchants, Sackville Street, Leeds, yesterday attained his 80th birthday and in celebration of this and his 50 years in business in the city his employees presented him with a barometer and case. Only last year Mr Fisher rode a push bike from Liverpool to Leeds."

When Greevz died in May 1931 his cremation ceremony was marked by the "Yorkshire Post", which also detailed the numerous organisations that attended. Marie took over the business which on her death in 1950 was in turn run by her surviving children.

Greevz left a published legacy of over a hundred pamphlets, articles and letters that remain uncollected and, nowadays, largely unread. Whilst no single piece may be revelatory, taken together his life and work evidences and illustrates a vital thread of practical, home grown English anarchism that can still amuse and inspire.

Dominance vs. Egoism
Peter McAlpine

1972

From *Invictus* No. 20 (April 11, 1972). Invictus was published by L. A. Rollins, author of *The Myth of Natural Rights* (Underworld Amusements, 2019). Peter McAlpine was the pseudononymous author of *The Occult Technology of Power* (Underworld Amusements, 2016). This text retrieved from the Libertarian Microfiche Project (libertarianmicrofiche.com).

Dominance and Submission versus Egoism

The following was written as a radio presentation for the "Voice of Reason" in Detroit (WABX). It was rejected because the Objectivist Steering Committee was not in agreement about the ideas presented.

The motive for the rebellion of young people against parental and institutional authority is well-known: young people are sick and tired of surviving by kissing ass. Infants come into the world completely at the mercy of their parents. To the infant it appears that his survival and well-being rests on his ability to elicit love from his parents. He soon discovers that the way to elicit "love" is to submit to his parents urge to dominate. The child thus learns to respond to his parents values. He learns that it is "cute" and therefore a means of survival to ape the subservient role.

The subservient role is nearly universal among toddlers, but soon the resentment and hatred that submission breeds creates a desire for the opposite, that is, dominance. Perhaps temper tantrums are the method by which the child first attempts to assume the dominant role.

Existing society can be described as a complex pecking order, designed to perpetuate the vicious circle of submission, resentment, and then, compulsion to dominate others which infects more people with the psychology of submission.

Society is divided into three major divisions: men, women, and children. Men dominate women and women dominate children. There is, of course, also a system of dominance and submission within these broad categories that is far too complex to describe at this time. Careful observation will reveal that the great bulk of people spend most of their time jockeying for position in various pecking orders. Politics, whether on the job, in the sphere of public office, or voluntary groups, is the euphemism people use to describe the quest for dominance and power.

Survival by dominance and submission systems is really a primitive Social system of trade that man shares with animals. Practically all animals that live in groups such as chickens, wolves, monkeys, and cattle have elaborate pecking orders that provide the group solidarity necessary for survival.

The submissive partner in any relation trades his self-respect, individuality, and self-assertiveness for protection and safety. The submitter says, "I am weak and therefore, no threat to you. I will satisfy your cravings and follow your orders. I'll kiss your ass as long as you let me live."

The dominant partner, on the other hand, trades the physical courage necessary for the defense of the weak for the pleasure and material advantage of being the master of slaves. The dominator says "As long as you are no threat I will keep you alive for my benefit."

This view of human society is grim indeed. No doubt it is this view of social reality that leads various submitting groups such as women, blacks, workers, and youth to rebel. Rebellion is an attempt to regain the self lost in the degradation of submissive behavior. Unfortunately, rebellious movements too often merely attempt to turn the tables by assuming the dominant role or make subservience to the collective universal as in socialism rather than attempt to banish dominance and submission from the social scene.

Fortunately, there is an ethical orientation that does not involve the mutual degradation of dominance and submission. That ethical outlook is egoism. The egoist does not live for others or ask others to live for him. He worships nothing above the self. He does not himself or expect others to trade away their self-respect for survival. The egoist must temporarily make terms with superior force, but never in his heart surrenders his life to another in honest submission. Egoism is the rejection of the "slave morality" which posits submission and meekness as a virtue as well as a rejection of the "master morality" that makes virtues out of exploitation, aggression, and brute strength. What would a society of egoists be like? It would be a society where autonomous individuals trade value for value, where forthright selfish trade in services and goods replaced the degrading transactions of dominance and submission, where the harmony of rational self-interest replaces the chaos of force and bureaucracy, where people do not set their calendars to satisfy so-called "social obligations," where there are no power lusters who juggle pacifying the masses against getting their own way, where there are no resentful, downtrodden masses who must trade in their self-esteem in order to live, where productive effort replaces the whining demand that self-sacrifice be rewarded, where people are equal in spiritual egoism, but unequal to the degree of their effort, ability, and luck, where supply and demand rather than government edict directs productive enterprise, and where individual rights are defended and aggression prohibited. This is egoist anarchy!

More Individualism
Mark A. Sullivan

Mark A. Sullivan was the editor of the New York gay egoist anarchist journal *The Storm* (1976), a periodical Peter Wilson later co-edited. *The Match* is one of the longest-running anarchist journals in-print, and is edited and published by Fred Woodworth. This letter was published a year before Sullivan's first issue of *The Storm* appeared.

EDITOR: —I would like to respond to the criticism of my letter in the March issue leveled by R. Yves Breton in the May issue.

First, I did NOT state, nor even imply, that under ALL circumstances "...ownership of what one uses and produces can only be realized by collective ownership of the factory by THE WORKER OF THAT FACTORY, no more nor less." I prefaced that remark with: (which R. Yves did NOT quote) "...it seems that, for the worker (note the context) the individualist goal of personal property can only be realized by some sort of active struggle with the system. Given that industrial production is necessarily a collective venture...." (again, note the context, R. Yves). How, in a factory geared to a minute division of labor, assembly lines, and massive machines, a worker can INDIVIDUALLY own his or her own tools, as E. Armand suggested, is beyond my comprehension (do the workers dismantle the machines in the evening and take the pieces with them to their separate homes?). Of course there is much individualistic argument in favor of dismantling, permanently, the stupefying factory system, and restoring (perhaps with more sophisticated individual tools) craft production. Given an Anarchistic society this would be possible, but at present we are prisoners of production systems we do not own nor control. Either we control the workshops or abandon them and recreate an entire productive system outside the present one. Certainly for most workers who cannot afford to quit their jobs, the first is the only alternative at this time. Should workers succeed in such a take-over, I would still not maintain that a free society is necessarily reached. Significantly, R. Yves Breton did not go on to quote my conclusion: "But no one should be forced to participate in the collective, nor be banned from individual enterprise."

I may be guilty of identifying workers' control of the workplace with syndicalism, as the latter term implies FEDERATION of industries as well as factory autonomy. Still there have been individualists who saw in syndicalism "A valid form of regaining one's property"— not the ONLY valid form, as R. Yves seems to imply as my meaning.

In this context, I would mention Malfew Seklew: "...I am an iconoclastic, atheistic, anarchistic, hedonistic individualist, with the social instinct well developed, and with syndicalistic solutions for the problem of poverty." ("Minus One" #34). Oscar Wilde and Guy Aldred advocated forms of collective ownership in order to lift the burden of material concerns from the stifled individualities of the working and exploiting classes. An ideal, perhaps, but an individualism that cannot include social cooperation is an undeveloped individualism in my opinion. Even the most extreme individualist, Max Stirner, advocated collective take-overs of The means of production, even communistic arrangements within the context of voluntary associations to better satisfy our HUMAN needs and give us time to realize our UNIQUE desires. In America, Emma Goldman and John Beverly Robinson, both influenced by Stirner, were able to believe that, economically, the interests of working people were similar enough to justify voluntary, collective, and federated running of all industries. Besides, even the skills and tools needed to survive alone, outside of society, were given to us by society itself. The benefits of human association and cooperation appeal to my interests as an individual. There is much egoistic reason to favor collective arrangements to satisfy common needs, rather than reliance upon often wasteful or exploitive competition.

"Finally, as regards competition once more, it has a continued existence by this very means, that all do not attend to their affair and come to an understanding with each other about it. Bread is a need of all the inhabitants of a city; therefore they might easily agree on setting up a public bakery. Instead of this, they leave the furnishing of the needful to the competitive. Just so meat to the butchers, wine to the wine-dealers, etc."

Peter Kropotkin? No, Max Stirner! Individualism IS the basis of true cooperation; as this primal Anarchist *par excellence* goes on to say:

"If I do not trouble myself about MY affair, I must be CONTENT with what it pleases others to vouchsafe me."
(*The Ego and His Own*, page 275).

Individualism and Property
Mildred J. Loomis
1965

From the British journal *Freedom: Anarchist Weekly*, Vol. 26 No.2, January 16, 1965. *Freedom* was started in 1886 by volunteers including Peter Kropotkin and Charlotte Wilson and continued with a short interruption in the 1930s until 2014 as a regular publication. Midlred J. Loomis was the right-hand of homesteader and agrarian philosopher Ralph Borsodi. She ran Borsodi's School of Living for many years and edited and published a sucession of journals for them.

Dear Editors,

I welcome the attempt to distinguish between individualist and communist anarchism, but so far the discussions in your paper have been too general. They spend too much time on generalities—on whether an individualist anarchist lacks altruism and whether the communist anarchist needs more self-expression, etc., etc.

I'm wondering whether others would agree that a major need is to discover the differences these two schools of anarchism have—both in philosophy and practice—toward land, money and goods. How do individualist anarchists propose to handle these basic economic realities; what plan do communist anarchists have? And is either group anywhere in the world actually implementing some anarchist policy regarding land, money and goods?

My friend Laurance Labadie, strong American individualist anarchist, points out the confusion in thought and practice from loosely lumping land, goods and money under the term "property". Most of us think of property as a thing, and we commonly say, "This house, this land, this car, is my property". But property correctly expresses a relationship between persons or between persons and objects. Property expresses a social policy, the essential fact of which is exclusion. It is more clear to say, "I have property in this land, in this car or this house". By which I mean I am protected in excluding others from this land, car or house.

Is it true that individualist anarchists stress this right of exclusion—that they do want to emphasize this right to their land, their houses and their cars? And that communist anarchists prefer to combine with others in the use of land, of goods and of an exchange media? (It goes without saying, of course, that both groups would want an equal access to these things. They would not want a monopolistic or privileged access to land, goods or money as exists in the capitalist world). But granted equal access, and freedom—is it a fact that communist anarchists prefer to hold property jointly and in combination? Is it true, as some individualist anarchists say, our sense of privacy, our individuality, our creativity and responsibility for our own actions is better obtained if we have individual use of land, property and money?

In either case, we all face the crucial questions: What gives us the right to exclude others from our house, land, car? How is land different from houses and cars?

Most people will agree that if an individual puts energy into producing a house or car, or in producing the medium (money) through which he gives value for it—that he thus earns the right to exclude others from them.

But how can you earn, in this fashion, the right to exclude others from land? Since land is a given, nothing you can do will produce it. Is it not in our laws that implement exclusion from land—more than we are actually using—that we find the first need for force? Is it not in granting privilege to persons to "enclose" more land than he actually needs that coercion is needed to exclude others who also "need" this basic source of life and sustenance?

American individualist anarchists have (and are) stressing a difference in the type of exclusion to produce goods from exclusion to land. In houses, cars and goods produced by human labour, this property or exclusion could be permanently at the discretion of the producer, or whoever had given acceptable value in exchange for it. In the case of non-man-made land, this exclusion would be contingent on the person's occupancy and acceptable use of that land.

These concepts are examined and elaborated in two studies from the School of Living, Brookville, Ohio: a new 200-page book, *Go Ahead and Live!* ($4) has chapters on it by Werkheiser and Labadie; and *Property and Trustery* by Ralph Borsodi is $1.00.

Sincerely,
(Mrs.) Mildred J. Loomis
Editor, *A Way Out*, Brookville, O.

Why I am a Right-Wing Anarchist
Robert Anton Wilson   1969

Excerpts from an essay by Robert Anton Wilson (1932–2007), writing as Ronald Weston, that appeared in *robertSPARK* magazine (Chicago, May 1969).

Robert Anton Wilson served as co-editor of the magazine *Balanced Living* in 1962. *Balanced Living* was founded by Ralph Borsodi, author of *This Ugly Civilization*. Wilson was an associate editor of Playboy magazine from 1965 to 1971. During that time he was amused and inspired by conspiracy-expose manuscripts mailed to the magazine. In 1975 he combined his interest in conspiracies (factual and fanciful), new religions (including the Discordianism of Greg Hill and Kerry Wendell Thornley), science fiction and right-wing anarchism into The *Illuminatus!* Trilogy, co-authored with Robert Shea.

Between 1978 and 2002, John Zube committed over five hundred thousand pages of rare libertarian, anarchist, free market and related materials to microfiche. In 2016, Kevin I. Slaughter purchased the only complete collection of Zube's "Peace Plans." These texts have passed from paper to microfilm to scanned images to online at the Libertarian Microfiche Project (LMP). While converting this issue of *robertSPARK* to microfiche, Zube mistakenly attributed the essay to Robert Shea. The website of Robert Anton Wilson links to a PDF of the microfiche at the website of Robert Shea—this PDF made from images by way of the LMP.

Most contemporary writers either think communist anarchism (Bakuninism) is the only form of anarchism; or, if they have heard of Right-wing (individualist) anarchism at all, they have the impression it is a freaky offshoot from the mainstream. Actually, individualist anarchism is the oldest form of anarchism, and, if there were such a thing as proprietorship in words, the school would have the clearest title to possession of the word "anarchy." Communist anarchism only arose after Bakunin attempted to synthesize the individualist anarchism of Proudhon with the socialism of Karl Marx. [...]

In 1832, [Josiah] Warren began publishing *The Peaceful Revolutioninst*—the first anarchist newspaper in the world. In it, he analyzed the causes of the failure of American democracy and predicted that the failure would grow steadily worse, as more and more wealth and power became centralized in fewer and fewer hands. He also analyzed the failure of [socialist experimental community] New Harmony, and foresaw the totalitarian tendency that future socialist experiments would necessarily develop. And he offered, as an alternative, the system which has become known as Right-wing, or individualistic, or Jeffersonian, or Warrenite anarchism, sometimes also called voluntary socialism or mutualism.

In the next decade, two other original thinkers, independent of Warren and of each other, came to the same conclusions in Europe–P. J. Proudhon, author of *What is Property?* and Max Stirner, author of *The Ego and His Own.*

In the more-than-a-century since then, we Right-wing anarchists have watched, bemused and wry, as every form of coercive, and violent, and totalitarian, and paranoid type of regimentation has been tried, under the banner of "socialism" and "the welfare of the people," and we are more convinced than ever that the Socialist State is a worse menace to mankind than even the Capitalist State. A system that produces Stalins and Berias is even more perverted than a system that produces Nelson Rockefellers and LBJs. Socialism is the counter-revolution.

What is the Right-wing anarchist alternative to Socialism and Capitalism? In a sentence, you could say it's the position of the Hopi Indians, who have a proverb that says: "No Man should be compelled to do that which goes against his heart." Benjamin Tucker, the most gifted writer in the individualist-anarchist tradition, put it this way: "Will you allow any form of coercion of the non-coercive individual? If so, you are an archist; if not, you are an anarchist."

Opening and Closing the Dil Pickle
Trevor Blake

2022

> "Cruel Tax Man Puts 'Kibosh' on Famous Bohemian Meetings"—*The Muscatine Journal*
> "Club Killed by Taxes"—*The Oakland Tribune*
> "Dill Pickle Club Gone"—*The Des Moines Tribune*

Newspapers across the land marked the closing of the doors of the Dil Pickle Club on July 8, 1921—one hundred years ago on this day. The Dil Pickle Club (so spelled in a painted sign above the entrance) was the creation of Jack Jones. Courting controversy above and beyond the neighboring Bughouse Square or Radical Book Shop, Jones welcomed every damned thinker he could find and anybody they brought with them. Malfew Seklew spoke there, and the Dil Pickle Press published an edition of *Might is Right* by Ragnar Redbeard in 1927. Poet Carl Sandburg and artist Stanislav Szukalski were no strangers to the Dil Pickle.

The Dil Pickle Club was located in Tooker Alley, Chicago. Tooker Alley, in turn, was accessed by an eighteen-inch gap between two buildings. The Club was located in at least two locations in Tooker Alley at different times. At some time it was in a building since torn down and replaced with a parking lot. At other times it was in "a barn" located in the alley. And at other times the Club seems to be hidden entirely from view, like Aladdin's cave. The *South Bend Tribune* of July 27, 1928 wrote: "The Dill Pickle Club in Tooker's Alley has the hardest door to find in Chicago. It's like playing 'Button, Button, Who's Got the Button' to find it. Entering Tooker's Alley in 'Towertown' (Chicago's Greenwich Village), the place resembles one solid wall. The door is a secret one which you have to find by moving your hand along the wall until you get a section that pushes in. It's a sort of hidden panel."

There's no getting in or getting out of the Dil Pickle Club now, save by the same imaginative spirit that animated the place while it was alive.

Free Spirits

Christmas a Joke!

Henry M. Tichenor

1914

Two poems from *Rhymes of the Revolution* (St. Louis: National Rip-Saw Publishing, 1914). Tichenor was the author of *Sorceries and Scandals of Satan*, (Baltimore: Underworld Amusements, 2010). His debate with egoist John Basil Barnhill was published as *Barnhill-Tichenor debate on Socialism* (St. Louis: National Rip-Saw Publishing, 1914).

The Red Pill Cure For Nightmares

I had a dream the other night that filled my soul with glory—t'was
    such a dream that I can't help but tell you folks the story.
I dreampt I lived in Crazy Land, where workin' folks are donkeys,
    who dig and sweat to beat the band to feed a lot of monkeys.
They starve and freeze and have no fun, their youngsters have no
    pleasure, while all the monks live lives of ease, like gentle-monks
    of leisure.
And I was feelin' awful glum—I dreampt I was a donkey, and life in
    Crazy Land is bum, unless you are a monkey—and I was wonder-
    in' what to do, and almost felt like croakin', when a troop of lions
    came along a laughin' and a jokin'.
"Come on!" they yelled, "come join the bunch, we're goin' to live in
    clover—we, too, were donkeys all our lives, but now the spell
    is over—we've found a little, round RED pill that beats your
    thoughts of dyin' and every ass that takes this pill becomes a
    FREE RED LION!"
I swallowed one of those RED pills—I was no more a donkey-I was a
    LION who refused to work for any monkey!

Christmas

He was taken out and crucified by rulers and their priests;
His followers were burned at stakes and fed to hungry beasts;
His call to Peace and Brotherhood—all that the sad world needs
Was hidden from the workers in a pile of pagan creeds;
And the race plunged on in darkness, just as it had before,
And for nineteen hundred years has damned the earth with Hate and
    War.
A world of "Peace" and "Brotherhood," where masters own the bread?
Christmas? Hell! What joke is this, in a land where Christ is dead?

"I" a poem
Enrique Magon

This poem was sent in a packet to our post office address, and the sender did not identify themselves. We thank this unknown contributor. Enrique Flores Magón (April 13, 1877–October 28, 1954) was a Mexican journalist and politician. He and his brother Ricardo Flores Magón espoused their own philosophy, *magonismo*. This poem was written by Enrique while in jail for distributing his anarcho-communist newspaper *Regeneración*.

I

Conditions would crush me,
Dull dunces would hush me,
If I were not I.
The world would enchain me,
Each fool would restrain me,
If I were not I.

Dear friends would ignore me
And blockheads would bore me
Until I should die;
But I know the rabble,
Their rant and their gabble,
And I am still I.

With punishments gloomy
They'd strive to undo me,
Because I am I.
I test them and try them
Then scorn and defy them,
For I must be I.

I cherish and love thee,
Think nothing above thee,
O glorious I!
Let others despise thee,
I honor and prize thee,
O infinite I!

L. A. Co. Jail, June 1st, 1916.

"I GO" a poem

Jack Jones

1927

From the second issue of the *Dil Pickler* (1927). Jack Jones was the founder of the Dil Pickle Club of Chicago. The Dil Pickle, in turn, was a hangout for Malfew Seklew and the publisher of *Might is Right* (1927).

I GO

I go slowly
In a slow way,
My means being lowly.
I go unbidden,
Yea even forbidden.
I go to discover—
I know not.
But I go,
For only can I know
By going.

—Jack Jones.

A Letter to the Editors of *Freedom*

Sidney E. Parker

From the British journal *Freedom: Anarchist Weekly*, Vol. 32 No. 5, Feb 27, 1971. *Freedom* was started in 1886 by volunteers including Peter Kropotkin and Charlotte Wilson and continued with a short interruption in the 1930s until 2014 as a regular publication, moving its news production online and publishing irregularly until 2016, when it became a bi-annual. Originally, the subtitle was "A Journal of Anarchist Socialism". The title was changed to "A Journal of Anarchist Communism" in June 1889.

Dear Editors,

Bill Dwyer gives a substantially correct report of what I recounted of my experiences as a member of a printing union 'chapel' (Freedom, 19.12.70). What he deduces from it, however, is wide of the mark.

Firstly, I do not maintain that 'the worker (whoever he is) is fitted only for obedience'. What I do maintain is that most workers (like most other people) have supported and defended authoritarianism and servility in the past, do so in the present and that, on the evidence of this, they will do so in the future. Every social upheaval so far has resulted in either the survival of the old authority or the creation of a new, and as far as I can see this is the inevitable outcome of all organized collectivities—no matter what names they are given. Bill Dwyer, like his utopian forebears, has confused 'the worker' as he is with 'the worker' as he would like him to be. He is, if you will pardon the philosophical pun, trying to deduce an 'is' from an 'ought'.

Because, however, this has been and is true of most workers, it by no means follows that all workers are incapable of transcending authoritarianism and becoming anarchists. A small minority in each generation do just this, as do a small minority of 'non-workers'. (Anarchism is an individual, not a class, phenomenon.) Secondly, what 'weakness' did Francis Ellingham show in my social pessimism? The only 'evidence' that he could offer to refute my view was that he believes that mankind can create the kind of world he would like to see by means of some unexplained (and, I suspect, unexplainable) process of concurrent and contagious spontaneity of the sort that will result in what Ellingham wants it to result in. Of course, any millenarian sect can claim the viability of their goal on this kind of 'evidence'. From Plymouth Brethren to Koreshanists—all can view the world as their oyster. More tough-minded folk, however, would demand better credentials than those so far offered.

Thirdly, I cannot see how I am being 'insulting' to point out what I think are the facts of the case. (F.E. is fond of derogatory labelling too. Because I have said most people appear to want a government of some kind or other he accuses me of saying they are 'stupid'. Not so. Some of the most ardent governmentalists are very intelligent persons. Intelligence is no more a monopoly of anarchists than is stupidity of anarchists.) If I claimed that on the basis of what I knew about Bill Dwyer I thought it unlikely he could run a mile in three minutes would he regard that as being 'insulting'? Emotive [illegible] of this kind is simply begging the question.

Finally, I have never claimed that 'no change' is possible. The world I live in now is in many ways not the world I lived in twenty years ago, nor is it the kind of world I will live in twenty years from now. My point is that what changes will take place are, on the basis of what is and has been in the sphere of social constraint, unlikely to bring about anarchy as a universal condition. For this reason anarchist individualists, such as I claim to be, will shape their perspectives accordingly. Anarchism as an individualism can survive such a reshaping. I am quite prepared to admit that those who regard anarchism as a socialism will reject my view, since their ideas cannot.

Yours Sincerely,
S.E. Parker
London, W.2

A new bibliography of the English-language books by Enrico Arrigoni. Because the publication dates aren't known for all the books, they have been listed in alphabetical order.

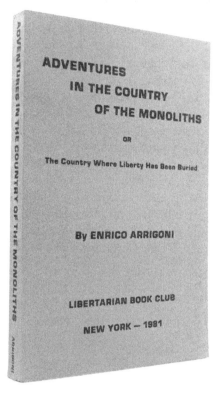

Adventures in the Country of the Monoliths: or, The Country Where Liberty Has Been Buried
Arrigoni, Enrico
New York: Libertarian Book Club, 1981
Paperback. 269p., wraps, 5.5×8.25 inches
Canary yellow wraps, interior professionally typeset.
Libertarian Book Club on cover and title page. Address given for LBC as "Box 842, General Post Office". No copyright statement or other information on verso of title page.
Back cover is blank.

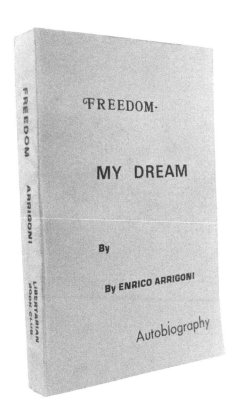

Freedom: My Dream
Arrigoni, Enrico
New York: Libertarian Book Club, [198-?].
Paperback. 440p., wraps, 5.5×8.25 inches
Light green wraps, text typeset by typewriter ragged right. Very
    small margins, inconsistent text block height.
Libertarian Book Club on spine and copyright page, though it lacks
    copyright statement.
Address for LBC given as "Now 339 Lafayette Street, Room 212",
    implying a recent move.
Back cover is blank.

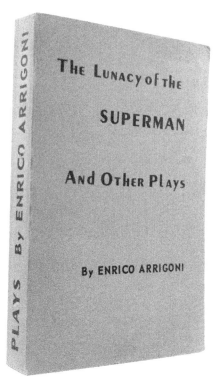

The Lunacy of the Superman and Other Plays
Arrigoni, Enrico
[No publisher information given], 1977
Paperback. [~600]p., wraps, 5.5×8.25 inches
Red lettering on pink wrap, "superman" in all caps.
Text on spine is bottom-up, in reverse of normal orientation.
Title page has an explicit statement that the book and contents are not copyrighted and "can be performed without permission or royalty payments." It further states that the book was "distributed free".
Below the table of contents is a statement that the book is printed on light yellow paper to prevent "bleed-through" on photocopies made for cast of a play.
Ten plays printed, folio resets for each play. Interior typeset by typewriter.
Back cover is blank.

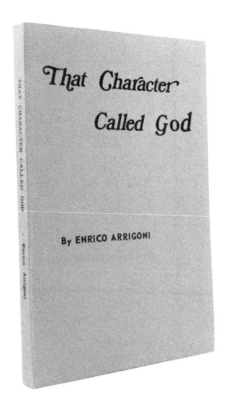

That Character Called God
Arrigoni, Enrico
[No publisher information given, no date of publication]
Paperback. 180p., wraps, 5.5×8.25 inches
Red lettering on canary yellow wrap. No publisher information or
    publication date is given.
Title page states "No Copyright". No content of verso of title page.
    No table of contents.
Professionally typeset in small point.
Back cover is blank.

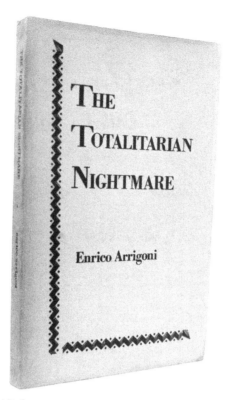

The Totalitarian Nightmare
Arrigoni, Enrico
Foreword by Paul Avrich
Culver City: Western World Press
Paperback. 285p., wraps, 5.5×8.25 inches
White wraps. Inside front cover gives notices of corrections on last
  two pages. Table of contents.
Copyright page, found after Foreword, states "First Printing
November 1975". Further states "published without copyright."

Photo of Benjamin R. Tucker
Dorlys
(no date)

This portrait of Tucker with a card to L. Labadie that reads: "I take pleasure in presenting this photo to Laurance Labadie, the only young person that I recall who, being the offspring of an avowed anarchist, finds his greatest satisfaction in continuing the battle, even though the cause be lost. More power to his elbow! Benjamin R. Tucker, Sept. 6, 1936."
Labadie Photograph Collection, University of Michigan.

ABOUT THE EDITORS

KEVIN I. SLAUGHTER (b. 1975) is a graphic designer and book publisher by vocation and intellectual dissident and misanthropologist by avocation.

Mr. Slaughter is the Archivist for the Sidney E. Parker Archives (sidparker.com) and the Benjamin DeCasseres website (benjamindecasseres.com). He is also the editor for the egoist journal *Stand Alone*, a mixed medium journal with over 80 issues published. In 2012 he edited *A Bible not Borrowed from the Neighbors: Essays and Aphorisms on Egoism*, retired from print in 2020. In 2023 he published his first authored book: *The Radical Book Shop of Chicago: In Which a Disaffected Preacher, His Blind Anarchist Wife, and Their Precocious Daughters Create an Important Hub of Literary, Bohemian, and Revolutionary Culture in Progressive-Era Chicago*.

Mr. Slaughter has lectured at Universities on the topic of Satanism, and an hour long presentation titled "Satanism as Weltanschauung: The Philosophy of the Church of Satan" is available on YouTube. Mr. Slaughter has been honored with the title of Magister in the Church of Satan. He has also won the Robert G. Ingersoll Oratory Award.

TREVOR BLAKE (b. 1966) is the author of *Confessions of a Failed Egoist*, *Dora Marsden Bibliography* and *The Eagle and the Serpent Index of Names*. He has written introductions to books by egoists including *The Gospel of Malfew Seklew* by Malfew Seklew, and both *The Gospel of Power* and *The Philosophy of Time* by Dora Marsden. He lives in Columbus, Indiana.

"At every turn in its thought, society will find us waiting."

SELECT TITLES AVAILABLE
FROM THE UNION OF EGOISTS

Hyde Park Orator Illustrated
Bonar Thompson
Trevor Blake (introduction)
6×9", 354 pages
ISBN-13: 978-1944651183

A Brave and Beautiful Spirit: Dora Marsden, 1882-1960
Les Garner
6×9", 486 pages
ISBN-13: 978-1944651145

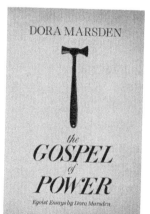

The Gospel of Power: Egoist Essays by Dora Marsden
Dora Marsden
Trevor Blake (editor)
6×9", 390 pages
ISBN-13: 978-1944651206

WWW.UNIONOFEGOISTS.COM

Made in the USA
Middletown, DE
14 October 2023

40612689R00119